The Assault on Bergen-op-Zoom, 1814

SIR THOMAS GRAHAM, 1ST BARON LYNEDOCH
GCB GCMG

The Assault on Bergen-op-Zoom, 1814

A British Army Defeat in Holland by Napoleon's French Forces

ILLUSTRATED

John Murray Graham
Alex M. Delavoye
Percy Groves
J. W. Dunbar Moodie
Sir John T. Jones

LEONAUR

The Assault on Bergen-op-Zoom, 1814
A British Army Defeat in Holland by Napoleon's French Forces
by John Murray Graham
Alex M. Delavoye
Percy Groves
J. W. Dunbar Moodie
Sir John T. Jones

ILLUSTRATED

FIRST EDITION

Leonaur is an imprint of Oakpast Ltd
Copyright in this form © 2018 Oakpast Ltd

ISBN: 978-1-78282-780-1 (hardcover)
ISBN: 978-1-78282-781-8 (softcover)

http://www.leonaur.com

Publisher's Notes

The views expressed in this book are not necessarily
those of the publisher.

Contents

Bergen-op-Zoom, 1814: An Overview

John Murray Graham

Soon after returning to England, from the Iberian Peninsula, Sir Thomas Graham found his eyesight and his general health so much improved, that he accepted an appointment to command a body of troops sent from this country to Holland, to assist the Dutch in their insurrection against the French rule. A Prussian force under General Bülow was to co-operate in South Holland for the same purpose.

In the beginning of January 1814, the French had evacuated all the fortified places in Holland, with the exception of the strong fortress of Bergen-op-Zoom and one or two other fortresses and had concentrated the strength of their troops in Antwerp, of which the veteran Carnot had been appointed governor. The British and Prussians having occupied Breda and Williamstadt made a forward movement in the direction of Antwerp. After some desultory fighting, and dislodging the enemy from his positions, a well-contested battle was fought on the 13th of January at Merxhem, near Antwerp. The French were driven from their intrenchments with the loss of a thousand men and retreated within the fortifications of Antwerp. (Sir T. Graham to Earl Bathurst, 14th January 1814; *Edinburgh Annual Register,* Appendix.)

To lay regular siege to Antwerp was an operation entirely out of the question for the allied force to undertake; but with the help of some Dutch mortars they established a small battery, and for three days bombarded the place. The attack was confined chiefly to the great basin of Antwerp and the ships of war within it. The efforts of the besiegers were, in a considerable degree, counteracted by the precautions of Carnot. Two or three small ships were sunk, and the French custom-house burned. Not having intended a regular bombardment of the town, while part of their ordnance had become unserviceable and their ammunition was failing, the allies desisted from their attack, (Sir

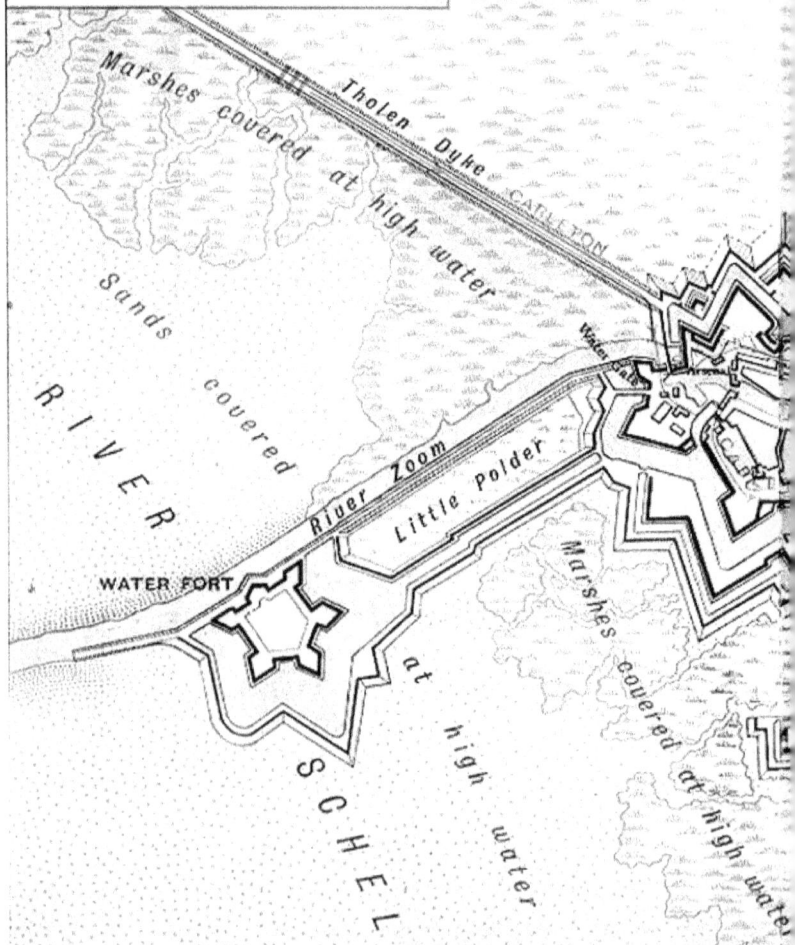

BERGEN-OP-ZOOM
March 8, 1814
Scale, 1:13,000

To Steenbergen

Zoom

LINES OF STEENBERGEN

HENRY

To Breda

MORRICE

Powder
Magazine
Modfilll

Steenbergen
Gate

Breda Gate

Fame Gate

Central
Square

Orange
Bastion

Antwerp
Gate

ENTRENCHED CAMP

MORRICE

MORRICE

COOKE

T. Graham to Earl Bathurst, 6th February 1814; *Edinburgh Annual Register*, Appendix); the Prussian force at the same time receiving orders to join the grand army which was then entering France. The British force under Sir Thomas Graham, augmented by reinforcements and a corps of Germans to about 9000 men, remained in cantonments on the north side of Antwerp, in readiness to protect the country against excursions from the French garrison.

Bergen-op-Zoom, the only place of consequence then remaining to the French in Holland, is one of the strongest fortresses in the Low Countries. Situated on a flat near the mouth of the Scheldt, its works were designed by the celebrated Cohorn. A stranger approaching the town might not discover its great strength until made aware of it by the winding of his carriage among the endless lines of outworks, bastions, moats, and drawbridges. It was garrisoned by upwards of 4000 French troops (of which about 2700 were effective), commanded by General Bizanet—a force inadequate to the manning of its extensive lines and outworks. Some of the defences were out of repair, and the wet ditches were frozen over. The native inhabitants, numbering about 6000—mostly seafaring people of a peaceful character—were favourable to any attempt to relieve them from the French yoke.

Such being the condition of matters at Bergen-op-Zoom, Sir Thomas Graham planned an assault of the place by surprise as the only mode of attack open to him under the circumstances. The troops destined for this service amounted to 3900, divided in four columns, commanded by General Cooke. Of these columns, two were to make their way by escalade at certain points of the rampart near the Antwerp Gate; another was to make a feint and diversion at the Steinberger Gate; the fourth was to enter by the Water Gate, at a place where the small River Zoom flows from the town into the harbour.

This access was fordable at low water, for which reason the attack was fixed for half-past ten o'clock on the night of the 8th of March. The instructions to the officers in command were, as soon as they reached the top of the rampart, to incline towards each other, unite and force open the Antwerp Gate. The operations commenced with the feint attack, which had the effect of drawing a large part of the garrison towards the Steinberger Gate. Of the columns that made the actual assault, two reached the ramparts near the Antwerp Gate by escalade—surmounting some unforeseen difficulties and having at several points to encounter a galling fire. Unfortunately, several of the officers, highest in command in their columns, fell early in the night—thus causing a defect in the communications and mutual understanding of all the troops. The column entering from the harbour by the Water Gate, keeping their footing with difficulty, gained the ramparts without the loss of a man, although, on separating to pass along the ramparts, they suffered from the garrison's fire. (Sir T. Graham's *Despatches*, 10th and 11th March 1814; *Edinburgh Annual Register*, 1814, Appendix. Alison's *History of Europe*, chap. Ixxiv. vol. x.)

Upwards of 2000 men were now upon the walls of an almost impregnable fortress. The enemy were surprised, and well-nigh prepared to surrender when it should be daybreak. The assailants had possession of nearly the whole of the ramparts and bastions, while some had actually entered the streets of the town. But fortune has much to say in war; and here she turned against the assailants. With the exception of General Cooke, the leading officers were killed or disabled; and there was felt the want of directing officers equal to the emergency. The garrison, recovering from their surprise, resumed the offensive; and, rallied by the governor and their officers, vigorously charged the assailants, already labouring under the disadvantages of want of leaders, confined space, and the mistakes and confusion incident to a night attack.

******

The Duke of Wellington, at the end of a despatch to Colonel Bunbury (1st April 1814, Gurwood, xi.), adverting to the issue of the attack on Bergen-op-Zoom, remarks that "Night attacks upon good troops are seldom successful;" an observation founded on and confirmed by previous historical instances—Stanhope's *Reign of Queen Anne*, 1702; Grote's *Greece*, part ii.

******

The Antwerp Gate, protected by its own strength and the fire of the garrison, could not be forced open; and the columns were thus prevented from uniting. Some of the soldiers got into spirit-shops, some were benumbed with cold, and all were more or less affected by that uncertainty and hesitation which are so fatal in military actions. No reinforcements arrived from without; and in this particular Sir Thomas Graham possibly trusted too much to the effect of surprise or panic upon the enemy, at the same time confiding more than circumstances allowed in the well-known courage of his troops, whose numbers were not more than equal to the number of the garrison.

As day broke, the guns of the place, where the situation permitted, were pointed against the assailants; and the governor, with full knowledge of the localities, directed the efforts of his men successively against the two corps of besiegers, who were divided from each other. After a desperate contest on the ramparts, and the loss of about 900 killed and wounded, the survivors of the British troops within the town were compelled to lay down their arms. The prisoners were exchanged the day after the assault of Bergen-op-Zoom (for siege it cannot be called) by convention with General Bizanet, whose humanity and courtesy are acknowledged in Sir Thomas Graham's despatch.

★★★★★★

To Earl Bathurst, 10th March 1814; *Edinburgh Annual Register*, 1814, Appendix. The narrative portion of this despatch is as follows: "It is unnecessary to state the reasons which determined me to make the attempt to carry such a place by storm, since the success of two of the columns, in establishing themselves on the ramparts with very trifling loss, must justify the having incurred the risk, for the attainment of so important an object as the capture of such a fortress. The troops employed were formed in four columns. No. 1, the left column, attacked between the Antwerp and Water Port Gates. No. 2 attacked to the right of the New Gate. No. 3 was destined only to draw attention by a false attack near the Steinberger Gate, and to be afterwards applicable, according to circumstances. No. 4, right column, attacked at the entrance of the harbour, which could be forded at low water, and the hour was fixed, accordingly, at half-past ten p.m. of the 8th inst.

> Major General Cooke accompanied the left column; Major-General Skerret and Brigadier-General Gore both accompanied the right column—this was the first which forced its way into the body of the place. These two columns were directed to move along the ramparts, so as to form a junction as soon as possible, and then to proceed to clear the rampart and assist the centre column, or to force open the Antwerp Gate. An unexpected difficulty about passing the ditch on the ice having obliged Major-General Cooke to change the point of attack, a considerable delay ensued, and that column did not gain the rampart till half-past eleven.
>
> Meanwhile, the lamented fall of Brigadier-General Gore and Lieutenant-Colonel Carleton, and the dangerous wounds of Major-General Skerret, depriving the right

column of their able direction, it fell into disorder, and suffered great loss in killed, wounded, and prisoners. . . . At daybreak, the enemy, having turned the guns of the place, opened their fire against the troops on the unprotected rampart; and the reserve of the 4th column (Royal Scotch) retired from the Water Port Gate, followed by the 33rd. The former regiment, getting under a cross fire from the place and Water Port redoubt, soon afterwards laid down their arms.

Major-General Cooke then despairing of success, directed the retreat of the Guards, which was conducted in the most orderly manner, protected by the remains of the 69th Regiment and of the right wing of the 55th (which corps repeatedly drove the enemy back with the bayonet), under the major-general's immediate direction. The general afterwards found it impossible to withdraw these weak battalions; and having thus, with the genuine feelings of a true soldier, devoted himself, he surrendered, to save the lives of the gallant men remaining with him. (The remainder of the despatch refers to the services of particular officers and troops.)

★★★★★★

It is within the scope of a memoir such as this, to record, in connection with the assault of Bergen-op-Zoom, two personal notices of Lord Lynedoch by Sir William Napier and by the Emperor Napoleon, as reported by Barry O'Meara. Sir William Napier, in a disquisition on Napoleon's instructions to his governors of fortresses, (*History of the Peninsular War*, vi.) which forbade the surrender of a fortress without having stood at least one assault, has the following passage:—

What governor was ever in a more desperate situation than General Bizanet at Bergen-op-Zoom, when Sir Thomas Graham, with a hardihood and daring which would alone place him amongst the foremost men of enterprise which Europe can boast of, threw more than 2000 men upon the ramparts of that almost impregnable fortress? The young soldiers of the garrison, frightened by a surprise in the night, were dispersed— were flying. The assailants had possession of the walls for several hours; yet some cool and brave officers, rallying the men towards morning, charged up the narrow ramps, and drove the assailants over the parapets into the ditch. They who could not at first defend their works were now able to retake them; and so completely successful and illustrative of Napoleon's principle was this counter-attack, that the number of prisoners equalled that of the garrison.

In Barry O'Meara's *Napoleon in Exile*, vol. 2, a conversation is reported in which the emperor, adverting to the English mode of besieging towns, observed, that:

> The storming of Bergen-op-Zoom was a most daring attempt, but that it ought not or could not have succeeded, the number of the garrison being greater than that of the assailants. (The garrison was nominally 4500 strong, but not all effective—Alison's *History*, chap. lxxiv. vol. x.)

O'Meara rejoined, that:

> The failure was in part to be attributed to one of the generals not having taken the precaution to communicate the orders which had been given to him to anyone else; so that, when he was killed or mortally wounded, the troops did not know how to act.

The Emperor replied, that:

> Even if no accident of the kind had occurred, the attempt ought not to have succeeded, unless the party attacked became as sometimes happened, panic-struck.

Napoleon then observed that General Graham had been commissary, (a mistake in point of fact), with the army at the time of his own first career of arms at Toulon. "A daring old man," the emperor said; and asked "if he were not the same who had commanded in the affair near Cadiz."

After the well-planned but unsuccessful attempt upon Bergen-op-Zoom, no operation of consequence occupied the small British Army in Holland during the spring of 1814; and it was ordered back to England on the occurrence of the events in France which terminated in the Peace of Paris and the abdication of Napoleon.

The Campaign in Holland from Sir Thomas Graham's Correspondence

Alex M. Delavoye

Two months had barely elapsed since his return home from Spain, when Sir Thomas Graham was again called upon to serve his country. The Dutch, rendered bold by the contemplation of the enormous odds arrayed against Napoleon, determined to throw off the yoke. They were without arms, and every fortress in Holland was in the hands of the French, but England promptly supplied their wants, and promised to send a force to assist them. With some difficulty, a corps of 8,000 men was gathered together, the command of which was pressed upon General Graham.

From Lord Bathurst.

Downing Street, Novr. 21st, 1813.

My dear Sir,

A deputation has arrived from Holland; they state that the French authorities have quitted it; that what there is of a French Army is evacuating it; that the States have resumed their functions in The Hague; that they are, however, without arms, but unanimous in resolution to rise, and as yet they have not got possession of any fortified place, for want of arms.

The government have determined to give them instant assistance. 20,000 stand of arms, with a proportional quantity of ammunition, has been for some time at the Nore to meet any sudden emergency. They will be ordered off by telegraph this evening.

We propose sending the Guards on Tuesday morning, and the remainder of the force, if possible, in the course of the week. We shall add about 1,500 marines. I am afraid much cannot be said in favour of the general discipline of this force, but we have done our best I may say, our all. Our dependence must be on the general spirit of the Dutch, and on a good choice of our officers. You will see, by the enclosed paper, the major-generals whom we have selected; they are on the spot and are very good. But it is most desirable that the commander-in-chief should be of established character, accustomed to act with foreign troops, and to struggle with all the difficulties to which this command may subject him.

He ought also to be one under whom our volunteering militia will feel confidence in acting whenever we may be enabled to avail ourselves of their services.

Under these circumstances you will, I trust, pardon my begging you to accept the command. I shall not press you to accept until you have seen me, as there may be many questions which you will like to ask; but I hope that this letter will induce you to set off very early from Brighton tomorrow, that I may have the pleasure of seeing you at this office in the course of the day. You will find me here from eleven to five.

I have the honour to be, my dear Sir, with great truth,

Your very sincere

Bathurst.

From Sir T. Graham to Lord Bathurst.

5, George Street, 22nd Novr. 1813.

My Lord,

I was just preparing to leave Brighton yesterday evening, when I had the honour of receiving your Lordship's letter by the messenger. Having an engagement on business of consequence at 10 o'clock this morning, I shall go down to your office between 11 and 12.

I must confess, my Lord, that the proposition in your Lordship's letter was so unexpected that, independent of all the circumstances which you refer to as natural objects of enquiry, I feel the greatest difficulty to bring my mind to think of the possibility of accepting this command unless I am to consider it to be an order, for, having requested to be relieved in the distinguished situation I held in the Peninsula on account of the state of my health, which I considered was such as to make it advisable that I should give up service at the time, I feel that, though now much better, I should be thought very inconsistent, and might even be suspected of having left the army rather on pretence of bad health than from its really being so.

I am well aware, however, that after the signal marks of favour I have received it is particularly my duty, as it has ever been my wish, to devote myself to the king's service whenever an opportunity of being of use occurred. I cannot help troubling your Lordship with this note for your consideration till I have the honour of seeing you.

> I have the honour to be, etc.,

Thos. Graham.

The arguments used by the War Minister had the effect of inducing Sir Thomas to accept the command, and on the same day he wrote to Lord Wellington apprising him of the fact.

To Lord Wellington.

London, 22nd Novr., 1813.

My Lord,

Your Lordship cannot be more surprised to hear that I am going with some troops to Holland than I am myself to find that it is so.

I certainly considered that it was quite understood that in leaving your army and the distinguished command I held in it I was relinquishing service forever, as I thought necessary from the state of my health; but having got better and being on the eve of going to Norfolk to shoot, I have been pressed into this service in way that precluded refusal.

All I could do was to bargain for a trial only, and I now sincerely regret having left the army before the conclusion of the campaign, as I should thereby have escaped this *corvée*, for I cannot look forward to its being otherwise than an irksome service, with scarce a chance of any material success; I shall be well pleased if we avoid disgrace. I shall not delay your Lordship longer as Lord Bathurst told me he was to write to you on the subject.

With sincere wishes for your Lordship's continued success and good health,

I have the honour to remain,

> Your Lordship's most obedient humble servant,

Thos. Graham.

Mansfield House, Novr., 22nd, 1813.

My dear Sir,

I met the Prince of Orange today at dinner and informed him of your having accepted the command. He expressed the greatest satisfaction at this intelligence. As he proposes to leave London on Wednesday will you forgive my suggesting to you to call upon him tomorrow. I have the honour to be,

    Yours very sincerely,

Bathurst.

Lieut.-General Sir Thomas Graham, K.B.

Downing Street, Decr, 1st, 1813.

My dear Sir,

I enclose to you a draft of the instructions for your comments; let me know if you wish to have any additions or further explanations.

A Mr. Grant has arrived from Holland, having left Scheveling early on Monday morning. He paints strongly, I understand, the enthusiasm of the people, and their total want of any means of defence. I will send him to you when I see him. I shall be obliged to you to send me back the draft of the instructions to my house if you can do so before half-past six, if not, to me at Fife house.

I have represented to the Duke of York the advantage which you would derive by having the local rank of General in Holland in your communications with the allied powers, and His Royal Highness will recommend it to the Prince Regent.

    I have the honour to be,

        Yours sincerely,

Bathurst.

While preparing again to quit England for his new scene of action General Graham received the pleasing intelligence that on the 7th of December, 1813, he had been unanimously elected a freeman of the incorporated trades of the City of Perth, and that, besides conferring these honorary distinctions on their gallant countryman, the above-mentioned incorporated trades were preparing to present him with a massive silver cup, which, when presented, bore the following inscription:—

To

GENERAL SIR THOMAS GRAHAM, K.B.

from

THE INCORPORATED TRADES OF PERTH,

in testimony of

Their respect for his Personal Virtues

and

Gratitude for his Public Services,

1 January, 1814.

From Lord Bathurst.

Downing Street, Decr. 14th, 1813.

My dear Sir,

The hereditary prince is to be put upon your staff, but it is by no means intended that you are to assign to him any division, unless any circumstances should hereafter arise to make it desirable in your opinion that such an arrangement should take place. At present there is no division vacant, nor do I foresee any vacancy. He will, on his landing, proceed to The Hague, and will probably have a command given him of some Dutch troops.

You are, I believe, sufficiently acquainted with the ingenuousness of his character, not to know how ready he is to accept advice, and his love for the British service. You will, I hope, therefore, enforce, what I have endeavoured to persuade him, that young troops, however zealous, are not in action to be depended upon, unless supported by a regular force, and that he must not lead his Dutchmen to battle unless he has some red coats near him.

I am,

Yours ever sincerely,

Bathurst.

From Lord Bathurst.

Downing Street, Decr. 14th, 1813.

My dear Sir,

I send you a duplicate of my letter which I wrote yesterday, and directed to Deal, as I find that you sailed yesterday. I received this morning several letters from Major-General Taylor. I have enclosed an extract of one which relates to an advance on Antwerp, by which it appears the Prince of Orange himself wishes

19

it. This removes all delicacy, as far as Dutch feeling is concerned. Of the practicability of the attempt, you must be the best judge. The information contained in other parts of Major-General Taylor's letter is either of too old a date to be of use or will be more amply afforded by Major-General Cooke. Major-General Taylor intended to go to the headquarters of Generals Witzing-erode and Bülow on the 13th instant, and after visiting those of General Benkendorf, will present himself to you, and will, I hope, be able to give you a satisfactory, at all events an accurate, statement of the respective force and disposition of the allied forces.

In your communications with the Prince of Orange, you will address him (and the hereditary prince) by the title of His Royal Highness.

I am, my dear Sir,

Yours very sincerely,

Bathurst.

General Sir Thomas Graham, K. B.

The British force arrived at the anchorage of Stavenine on the 17th of December and disembarked on the island of Tholen as rapidly as circumstances would allow. General Graham at once placed himself in communication with Generals Bülow and Benkendorf, the Prussian and Russian commanders, with a view to concerting measures for an active co-operation, being too weak to undertake any offensive operation by himself.

The necessary supplies of material were detained by contrary winds and did not arrive for some time after the landing of the troops, who were consequently unable to move. By degrees, however, the small army was put on an efficient footing, but before anything could be attempted against the enemy, Sir Thomas determined to revictual both Willemstadt and Breda—the latter, at that time, threatened by a French corps of about 7,000 men, which was daily expected to advance against it.

Towards the end of the month, General Benkendorf, whose headquarters were at Breda, signified to the British Commander his intention of withdrawing his corps in accordance with orders received from Marshal Blücher, who intended to cross the Rhine on the 31st. Should this movement take place, Sir Thomas Graham would, of necessity, be forced to detach troops from his small force to garrison the place until he could be relieved by Prussian troops or some of the newly-raised Dutch levies.

To General Benkendorf.

Willemstadt, 26 Decr., 1813.

Mon Général,

Je viens d'avoir l'honneur de recevoir la lettre de votre Excellence d'hier. C'est la nouvelle la plus fâcheuse possible pour moi, vu la nécessité absolu que les circonstances m'impose pour faire tout ce qui dépend de moi de défendre cette place de Willemstadt comme poste de mer et entrepôt de tout ce qui doit arriver de l'Angleterre à toute outrance. Je ne pourrais faire beaucoup pour Breda, mais je désirerais faire tout ce que je pourrais pour l'approvisioner pour deux mois, en y plaçant un peu d'infanterie, mais au moins de huit jours je ne pourrais pas être assuré de pouvoir envoyer ce convoi. J'espère donc que votre Excellence en tout cas ne sera pas obligé de quitter Breda avant ce terme. En attendant je hâterai tout le plus que je pourrais. Nous n'avons pas un homme ni cheval de cavalerie encore. Il y a d'artillerie qu'on débarque actuellement.

    J'ai l'honneur, etc.,

Thos. Graham.

Translation

Willemstadt, Dec. 26, 1813.

My General,

I have just received the honour of receiving your Excellency's letter of yesterday. This is the most unfortunate news possible for me, given the absolute necessity that circumstances impose on me to do everything that depends on me to defend this place of Willemstadt as a post office and warehouse of everything that must happen from England to all excess. I could not do much for Breda, but I would like to do everything I can to supply it for two months, with a little infantry, but at least eight days I could not be sure I could send that convoy. I hope, therefore, that your Excellency will not be obliged to leave Breda before this term. In the meantime, I will hurry as much as I can. We do not have a man nor cavalry horse yet. There is artillery being landed now.

    I have the honour, etc.,

Thos. Graham.

Eager to share in the general move on Paris, the Russian general could not be induced to stay longer than the 2nd of January, 1814, on which day Major-General Gibbs, with the 33rd, 54th, and 56th Regiments, was sent to take his place.

To General Bülow.

Klundert, 1er Janvier, 1814.

Monsieur le Général,

J'espère que votre Excellence saura déjà longtemps avant l'arrivé de cette lettre à votre quartier générale que j'ai déjà prévenu le désir de votre Excellence, mais j'espère toujours que votre Excellence remplacera par d'autres troupes celles que j'enverrai à Breda et que je ne pourrais pas y laisser. Je viens de savoir par une lettre de Milord Clancarty que le Prince "d'Orange fait marcher sur Breda 1,800 hommes de nouvelle levée, et que d'autres les suiveront de près. Je prierais votre Excellence de vouloir bien agréer l'assurance de la haute considération avec laquelle j'ai l'honneur d'être, etc.

Thos. Graham.

P.S.—Les trois bataillons du Général Gibbs ne monteront qu'à mille baionettes."

Translation

Klundert, January 1st, 1814.

General,

I hope that your Excellency will know already long before the arrival of this letter to your headquarters that I have already informed your Excellency's desire, but I still hope that your Excellency will replace by other troops those which I will send to Breda and I cannot leave there. I have just learned from a letter from Milord Clancarty that the Prince of Orange is marching 1,800 men on Breda, and that others will follow them closely. I would ask your Excellency to accept the assurance of the high consideration with which I have the honour to be, and so on.

Thos. Graham.

P.S.—The three battalions of General Gibbs will only mount a thousand bayonets.

To the foregoing request General Bülow acquiesced so promptly that within a week the three English regiments were able to be withdrawn, and he had made Breda his headquarters. Two regiments of cavalry having by this time joined the English force, and the troops being now fairly equipped, General Graham was enabled to consent to take part in a forward movement in the direction of Antwerp, which General Bülow proposed should commence on the 11th.

To Lord Bathurst.

Headquarters, Calmthout,

14th January, 1814.

My Lord,

General Bülow, Commander-in-Chief of the 3rd corps of the Prussian Army, having signified to me that on the morning of the 11th inst. he was to carry into execution his intention of driving the enemy from their position at Hoogstraten and Wortel-on-the-Merk in order to make a reconnaisance on Antwerp, and that he wished me to cover the right of his corps, I moved such parts of the two divisions under my command as were disposable from Roosendaal, and arrived here at daybreak on the morning of the 11th.

The enemy were driven back from West Wezel, Hoogstraten, etc., after an obstinate resistance, by the Prussian troops to Braaschat, Westmalle, etc.

Dispositions were made to attack them again the following day, but they retired in the night of the 11th, and took up a position near Antwerp, the left resting on Merxem.

General Bülow occupied Braaschat in force that evening (the 12th). I moved to Capelle on the great road from Bergen-op-Zoom to Antwerp to be ready to co-operate in the intended attack yesterday.

Major-General Cooke's division remained in reserve at Capelle, and Major-General McKenzie's moved by Ekeren and Douc towards Merxem, so as to avoid both the great roads occupied by the Prussians.

While the Prussians were engaged considerably more to the left, an attack on the village of Merxem was made by Colonel Macleod's brigade, led by himself in the most gallant style, and under the immediate direction of Major-General McKenzie.

The rapid but orderly advance of the detachment of the 3rd battalion of the Rifle Corps, under Captain Fullerton's command, and of the 2nd battalion 78th, commanded by Lieut.-Colonel Lindsay, supported by 2nd battalion 25th, commanded by Major MacDonell, and by the 33rd, under Lieutenant-Colonel Elphinstone, and an immediate charge with the bayonet by

23

the 78th, ordered by Lieutenant-Colonel Lindsay, decided the contest much sooner and with much less loss than might have been expected from the strength of the post and the numbers of the enemy.

Colonel Macleod received a severe wound through the arm in the advance to the attack but did not quit the command of the brigade till he became weak from loss of blood.

I am happy to think that the army will, probably, not be long deprived of the valuable services of this distinguished officer.

The enemy were driven into Antwerp with considerable loss, and some prisoners were taken.

I have the greatest satisfaction in expressing my warmest approbation of the conduct of all these troops. No veterans ever behaved better than these men, who then met the enemy for the first time.

The discipline and intrepidity of the Highland battalion, which had the good fortune to lead the attack into the village, reflect equal credit on both officers and men.

The same spirit was manifested by the other troops employed.

Two guns of Major Fyer's brigade were advanced in support of the attack, and by their excellent practice soon silenced a battery of the enemy.

The 52nd Regiment, under the command of that experienced officer, Lieut.-Colonel Gibbs, was afterwards moved into the village of Merxem, in order to cover the withdrawing of the troops from it, which was ordered as soon as the Prussian column arrived by the great road, the head of which had already driven in the outposts when our attack began.

Lieut.-Colonel Gibbs remained with the 52nd and 3rd battalion 95th till after dark.

This reconnaissance having been satisfactorily accomplished, the Prussian troops are going into cantonments, and this corps will resume nearly those it occupied before.

The severity of the weather has been excessive; the soldiers have borne it with great cheerfulness and patience, and I hope will not suffer very materially from it. I send enclosed a return of killed and wounded.

I have the honour, etc.,

Thos. Graham.

From Lord Bathurst.

Downing Street, Janry 28th, 1814.

My dear General,

I just write a line to tell you that we have not heard of you since the 10th. Colonel Bloomfield tells me he saw a copy of your despatch to me in the hands of Lord Clancarty some days ago, but neither the original nor the copy has arrived. I am happy, however, to hear that your movement on the 11th, 12th, and 13th was satisfactory, as far as it went. I have seen General Bülow's account to the King of Prussia, which speaks very handsomely of your co-operation.

I am, my dear General, etc.,

Bathurst.

Nothing of any importance occurred for some time after this skirmish; the troops were employed at drill, and their chiefs in awaiting anxiously, but vainly, for siege artillery and rockets, which report said had been shipped. They had not, however, arrived by the end of the month, when General Bülow again expressed his intention of making another attempt against Antwerp. The troops left their cantonments on the 27th, and on the 31st were before the town, when the village of Merxem having been retaken, batteries were thrown up, from which to shell, and, if possible, burn the fleet in the basin, with what result the following letter will show.

To Lord Cathcart.

Merxem, 5th Febry., at night.

My dear Brother,

I write you two lines by another officer going to the Austrian headquarters, to tell you that we cannot burn this fleet, our means in mortars and ammunition being too small for the undertaking where the enemy have so many men to employ in extinguishing fire whenever it breaks out. The easterly winds detained all the great ordnance train, rockets included, at home, and the ice in the river at Willemstadt prevented our getting the small ordnance equipment that had arrived, so that we were obliged to depend chiefly on such Dutch and French mortars as we could pick up.

The shells bad, the fuses worse, so that the practice could not be good. We have this evening expended our last shell, and though several ships were on fire, we have had the mortification to see that, notwithstanding a good breeze, the enemy was able to smother it. General Bülow has, too, received orders to advance, to favour the general movement, and for the present we must give the thing up, after having deserved success from the immense exertions made by the troops, and particularly by the two branches of the Ordnance Department. We shall remain for some time in this country, however, that is between this and Breda, to keep up communication, etc.

Many people expect that either by a great battle, or by negotiation, a general peace will soon take place. I shall not be sorry for my own part to have this service over, which I undertook reluctantly, and from which there never was any prospect of gaining any credit—the number and composition not admitting such an expectation. *Adieu.* All this time I forgot to say that a very fine young man, Lieut.-Col. Prince Reuss, in the King's German Legion (formerly in the Austrian cavalry), is the bearer. He served with great distinction with us in Spain where I saw a great deal of him. I beg most especially to recommend him to your notice.

God bless you all. Ever affectly yours,

T. Graham.

To Lord Bathurst.

Merxem, 6th February, 1814.

My Lord,

I should have been happy to have had to announce to your Lordship that the movement on Antwerp, fixed by General Bülow for the 2nd instant, had produced a greater effect, but the want of time, and of greater means, will account to your Lordship for the disappointment of our hopes of more satisfactory result, for General Bülow received (after we had got the better of all the great obstacles in the way of taking up a position near the town) orders to proceed to the southward, to act in concert with the Grand Army, and the state of the weather for some time back not only prevented my receiving the supplies of ordnance and ordnance stores from England, but rendered it impossible to land much of what was on board the transports at Willemstadt, the ice cutting off all communication with them.

I have, however, sincere pleasure in assuring your Lordship that the service was conducted by the officers at the head of the different departments with all the zeal and intelligence possible. To make up for the want of our own artillery, all the serviceable Dutch mortars, with all the ammunition that could be collected, were prepared at Willemstadt; and on the evening of the 1st, the troops of the 1st and 2nd Divisions that could be spared from other services were collected at Braaschat, and next morning this village (fortified with much labour ever since our former attack) was carried in the most gallant style in a much shorter time and with much less loss than I could have believed possible.

Major-General Gibbs, commanding the 2nd Division (in the absence of Major-General McKenzie confined by a dangerous fall from his horse), ably seconded by Major-General Taylor, and by Lieut.-Colonel Harris, commanding Major-General Gibbs' brigade, conducted this attack, in which all the troops concerned behaved with the usual spirit and intrepidity of British soldiers.

I feel particularly indebted to the officers already named, and also to Lieut.-Colonel Cameron commanding the detachment of the three battns. of the 95th, to Lieut. Colonel Hompesch with the 25th Regiment, Major A. Kelly with the 54th, Lieut.-Colonel Brown with the 56th, and Major Kelly with the 73rd, for the distinguished manner in which these corps attacked the left and centre of the village, forcing the enemy from every stronghold, and storming the mill battery on Ferdinand's dyke; while Major-General Taylor, with the 52nd under Lieut.-Colonel Gibbs, the 35th under Major Macalister, and the 78th under Lieut.-Colonel Lindsay, marching to the right, and directly on the mill of Ferdinand's dyke, threatened the enemy's communication from Merxem towards Antwerp.

Two pieces of cannon and a considerable number of prisoners fell into our hands. No time was lost in marking out the batteries which by the very great exertions of the artillery under Lieut.-Colonel Sir George Wood, and the Engineers under Lieut.-Colonel Carmichael Smyth, and the goodwill of the working parties, were completed and armed by half-past three of the 3rd. The batteries opened at that hour.

During the short trial of the fire that evening, the defective state of the Willemstadt mortars and ammunition was too visible. Our means were thus diminished, and much time was lost, as it was not till 12 at noon on the 4th that the fire could be opened again. That day's fire disabled five of the six 24-pounders.

Yesterday the fire was kept up all day. The practice was admirable, but there was not a sufficient number of shells falling to prevent the enemy extinguishing fire whenever it broke out among the ships, and our fire ceased entirely at sunset yesterday. It is impossible for me to speak too highly of the indefatigable exertions of both branches of the Ordnance Department.

I have much reason to be satisfied with the steadiness of the troops, and the attention of the officers of all ranks during the continuance of this service.

Detachments of the Rifle Corps did the most advanced duty under the able direction of Lieut.-Colonel Cameron, in a way that gave security to the batteries on Ferdinand's dyke; and though this line was enfiladed, and every part of the village under the range of the enemy's shot and shells, I am happy to say the casualties on the whole have not been numerous.

As soon as everything is cleared away, we shall move back into such cantonments as I have concerted with General Bülow.

I cannot conclude this despatch without expressing my admiration of the means in which General Bülow formed the disposition of the movement and supported this attack.

The enemy were in great force on the Deurne and Berchem roads but were everywhere driven back by the gallant Prussians, though not without considerable loss.

I have the honour,
    etc., etc., etc.,

Thos. Graham.

P.S.—His Royal Highness the Duke of Clarence returned from The Hague on the 1st inst. and has accompanied this advance on Antwerp.

From Lord Bathurst.
Downing Street, 15th Febry., 1814.

Sir,

I have the honour to acknowledge the receipt of your despatch of the 6th instant, reporting your proceedings against Antwerp, and I am to acquaint you that your conduct on this occasion has been entirely approved of by His Royal Highness the Prince Regent.

His Royal Highness has commanded me to desire you will express his approbation of the gallantry and spirit displayed by Major-General Gibbs, Major-General Taylor, Lieut.-Colonel Harris, and the several officers and soldiers engaged in the attack on the village of Merxem, and subsequent operations detailed by you.

His Royal Highness has likewise observed with much satisfaction the indefatigable exertions of the artillery and engineers.

I have the honour to be,

Sir,

Your obedient servant,

Bathurst.

General Sir Thomas Graham, K.B.

From the Duke of York.

Horse Guards, 15th February, 1814.

Sir,

Colonel Torrens having laid before me your letter of the 7th instant, covering the copy of your despatch of the 6th to Earl Bathurst, with an account of your late proceedings before Antwerp, I avail myself of the earliest opportunity of expressing my full approval of the judicious arrangements which you made for the execution of that service, and my satisfaction at the gallant and steady conduct of the troops under your orders, being convinced that your not having had complete success is to be attributed to circumstances which you could not possibly control.

I am,

Sir,

Yours,

Frederick.

General Sir Thomas Graham, K.B.

The allied forces now settled down to watch the fortresses of Antwerp and Bergen-op-Zoom, and to prevent their garrisons from being reinforced. On the 19th a strong Dutch brigade was joined to the British force, and further reinforcements were expected. As his strength increased, General Graham became anxious to again attempt the destruction of the fleet at Antwerp, and arrangements were being made between him and General Bülow for that purpose, when the latter received orders to move his corps southward. Alone, the number of the English was barely sufficient to maintain the blockade of the fortress, and therefore, all idea of assuming the offensive had to be abandoned.

By the end of February Sir Thomas had succeeded in getting his force thoroughly equipped and entertained no doubts of being able to hold his ground against all the French troops then in Holland. Such a state of inaction, however, was entirely foreign to his nature and his demands for an addition to his force, to enable him to strike a blow, became more and more urgent.

On the 18th, the Duke of Saxe Weimar informed the English General, through Major Stanhope, his A.D.C., that he had also been ordered to join the grand army. This movement by withdrawing the force at Lin, entirely disconnected the British corps, and left his flank uncovered. Major Stanhope was at once ordered to proceed to the Crown Prince of Sweden (Marshal Bernadotte) and to request reinforcements. He met the Prince at Cologne, and in reference to meeting states:—

I immediately waited on the Crown Prince, and had interesting conversations with him, which I am enabled to state with great exactness, having taken memoranda on leaving him after each interview.

On being shown into a room where the prince was in conversation with another officer, I delivered him the letter from General Graham, saying—"your Royal Highness is perhaps already acquainted with the intended advance of the Duke of Saxe Weimar." The prince said he was—"*vous venez donc me demander des renforts. J'aurai le plus grand plaisir en les envoyant au Général Graham qui est un homme trop estimable, trop Europié, vous me comprenez, qu'il est trop bien connu en Europe, que son caractère doit perdre faute des moyens. Je lui enverrai le corps du Général Walmoden qui est déjà sous la solde de l'Angleterre.*" ("you come to ask me for reinforcements. I will have the greatest pleasure in sending them to General Graham, who is too estimable, too European, you understand me, that he is too well known in Europe, that his character must be lost for lack of means. I will send him the corps of General Walmoden who is already under the pay of England.")

The prince then asked me to dinner next day, and I took my leave.

I dined with the prince; the dinner lasted a considerable time no general conversation, but everyone talking to his neighbour. After dinner the prince retired into his closet and sent for Mr. Thornton and me. He gave me the answer, saying, that he did not express himself in detail about the reinforcements, leaving me to state that Count Walmoden would immediately receive orders to march on Holland. Some conversation ensued as to the best point to direct them on, and as to the rank of General Graham. On my expressing to him General Graham's regret at not being able personally to pay his respects to him, the prince said, "*Mais, mon Dieu, cela est impossible! J'aurais le plus grand plaisir d'exprimer de bouche les sentimens que j'ai pour le Général Graham, non seulement quant au rapport de sa gloire militaire, non comme Anglais, mais comme Européan, mais pour ses qualites personelles. Dites-lui je vous prie que j'irai dix lieues pour rencontrer ce digne second de Lord Wellington. Voilà des bons Généraux. Si Lord Wellington était à la tête des armées alliés, Buonaparte serait perdu sans remède. Mais j'espère que, quatre mois plus tard ou quatre mois plus tot, l'Europe sera "sauvé. Ce sont vous autres qui l'ont sauvé en Espagne au moins qu'ici avec quelque bêtise on ne perd pas le jeu.*"

("But, my God, that's impossible! It would be my great pleasure to express the sentiments I have for General Graham, not only as to the relation of his military glory, not as an Englishman, but as a European, but for his personal qualities. Tell him, I beg you, that I will go ten leagues to meet this worthy second of Lord Wellington. These are good generals. If Lord Wellington were at the head of the allied armies, Buonaparte would be lost without remedy. But I hope that four months later or four months earlier, Europe will be saved. It was you who saved it in Spain, at least here with some foolishness we do not lose the game.")

While waiting for the promised reinforcements Sir Thomas Graham was astonished to receive a notification from the Secretary of War, informing him that his corps would probably have to be broken up for service in other parts.

From Lord Bathurst.

Secret.   War Department,
                                              London, 28th Febry., 1814.
Sir,
The circumstances of the war make it appear probable that

His Majesty's Government will find it advisable, within a short time, to break up the army which is employed at present under your command, and to direct that a large proportion of the troops should proceed direct from Holland to North America. You will receive further instructions before it will be necessary to make any communication upon this subject to the troops, or to separate from the rest the battalions which I have specified, but it is desirable that you should be prepared to detach these battalions upon the shortest notice, and to cause them to embark with their baggage and camp equipment on board the troop ships and transport, which may be sent to Helvoet to receive them.

I consider it advisable also to apprise you that in the event of your army being broken up, the greater part of the Foot Guards, under your command, will be sent to reinforce the army under the command of Lord Wellington, and the brigade of Foot Guards will be required accordingly to embark immediately after the force I have mentioned above, as being destined for North America.

I have the honour to be,
>   Sir,
>   Your most obedient humble servant,
>   Bathurst.

General Sir Thomas Graham, K.B.

This unexpected intelligence made General Graham more than ever desirous of getting possession of one, at least, of the many strongholds held by the enemy before the means of so doing were taken from him. Early in March he was informed that a large body of Hanoverian troops might be expected to join him shortly; but experience had taught him that weeks might pass before he could receive their help, consequently if anything was to be done it must be done at once.

> *From the Duke of Clarence.*
> Hague, March 5th, 1814.

Dear Sir,

Last night I received yours of 3rd instant and its enclosed from the Crown Prince, who writes as he acts. I send a copy of it to the Duke of Saxe Weimar and request you will forward the letter.

I cannot make out where the French came from that forced

the Prussian force at Courtray; if they reinforce Antwerp I am afraid you must remain inactive, yet I hope shortly the Hanoverians will join our troops.

Lord Clancarty is endeavouring to put life into the Dutch exertions, and to clothe the regiments in and about Breda. The Prussian officer, Major Dumouslier, and myself are also supporting his Lordship, and I am, at last, inclined to think things will proceed faster; they really have three-and-twenty thousand troops, and we have made the prince acknowledge that he has complete uniforms for sixteen thousand men, which he intended for the Militia that does not yet exist. The regiment of Nassau Wildberg, being perfectly ready for service, ought to join our troops at once, as should the Dutch regiment, hourly expected from Yarmouth, and a regiment now on the march from Germany; they also promised another brigade of four thousand infantry, entirely and completely equipped, to join the British before the end of the month.

I have by the last post received directions to return to England and am now waiting at this place for the ship to carry me home. I cannot leave Holland without returning you my sincere thanks for your kindness and attention to me during the different times I had the advantage of being at the British headquarters. I lament the exertions of the Dutch do not keep pace with your earnest wishes and desire of being useful to both countries. Should my destination be again changed I shall write, and hope in that case to be present at the capture of Antwerp. For the present, *Adieu*. God bless and preserve you, and ever believe me,

Dear Sir,

Yours sincerely,

William.

The great desire of the British Government was that Antwerp should be wrested from Napoleon, as he had positively refused to allow it to be included among those places which it was proposed should be given up by France. While making every effort to carry out these wishes by urging upon the Dutch and Hanoverian Governments the necessity for sending troops to assist in the undertaking, Sir Thomas Graham received information concerning Bergen-op-Zoom, which was sufficiently reliable to induce him to attempt the capture of that place by a *coup de main*.

The despatches and letters which follow describe fully the operation, which has been justly termed, "one of the most daring enterprises that have ever been undertaken."

Orders for the Attack on Bergen-op-Zoom.

March 8th, 1814.

The Pellik water or centre attack will be made by the undermentioned regiments, under the command of Lieut.-Colonel Morrice, 69th Regiment, *viz.*, 55th and 69th Regiments, to be supported by the 33rd Regiment. These regiments will be conducted from Huybergen by the bearer and will march as soon as possible after the receipt of this order. Proper officers to point out the places to be attacked will meet the column on its march. Lieut.-Colonel Morrice will give instructions to the 33rd Regiment, which is to support his attack, in order that this regiment may at once avail itself of any opportunity of profiting by any impression made by the attacking party.

Lieut.-Col. Smith, of the Royal Engineers, will make the necessary arrangements for attaching officers and men of his department to conduct this attack, and for the supply of scaling ladders and other means necessary.

The centre attack, having forced its way into the place, will immediately gain the rampart and put itself in connection, as soon as possible, with the troops which have attacked to its right and left, and be in readiness for any further operations against the enemy which may be necessary.

In order to avoid any mistakes that might arise from not being able to distinguish our own troops clearly the instant any men are perceived, the watchword 'Orange Boven' will be loudly called out, which will be answered by 'God save the King.'

Should the centre attack succeed in entering the place before the other attacks, Lieut.-Colonel Morrice will take measures to facilitate their entry by moving to his left along the rampart. The Halteren attack, consisting of the 44th Regiment and flank companies of the 21st and 37th Regiments, supported by the Royal Scots, will assemble at the junction of the two dykes at 9 o'clock (p.m.).

The south-west or left attack, consisting of 1,000 guards under Lord Proby, will be met by a guide at Borgerhet, and be led by him to the point of attack.

Major-General Skerrett will be pleased to order the following regiments, which are to attack on the side of Halteren, to assemble at that place as soon as possible:—

44th Regiment.

Flank Companies 21st & 37th

To be supported by the Royal Scots, which are now in that neighbourhood. The troops will be placed under the orders of Lieut.-Colonel the Honourable G. Carleton, of the 44th Regiment.

The above troops will march from Halteren so as to arrive at the two dykes next the Scheldt precisely at 9 o'clock (p.m.), when they will be met by the guides who are to conduct them to the point of attack.

To Lord Bathurst.

Headquarters, Calmthout,
10th March, 1814.

My Lord,

It becomes my painful task to report to your Lordship that an attack on Bergen-op-Zoom, which seemed at first to promise complete success, ended in failure, and occasioned a severe loss to the 1st Division and Brigadier-General Gore's brigade.

It is unnecessary for me to state the reasons which determined me to make the attempt to carry such a place by storm, since the success of two of the columns in establishing themselves on the ramparts, with very trifling loss, must justify the having incurred the risk for the attainment of so important an object as the capture of such a fortress.

The troops employed were formed in four columns. No. 1, the left column, attacked between the Antwerp and Waterport gates. No. 2 attacked to the right of the Woir gate. No. 3 was destined only to draw attention by a false attack near the Steenberg gate, and to be afterwards applicable, according to circumstances. No 4, right column, attacked at the entrance of the harbour, which could be forded at low water, and the hour was fixed accordingly at half-past ten, p.m., of the 8th instant. Major-General Cooke accompanied the left column; Major-General Skerrett and Brigadier-General Gore both accompanied the right column.

This was the first which forced its way into the body of the place.

These two columns were directed to move along the rampart, so as to form a junction as soon as possible, and then to proceed to clear the rampart and assist the centre column, or to force open the Antwerp gate.

An unexpected difficulty about passing the ditch on the ice having obliged Major-General Cooke to change the point of attack, a considerable delay ensued, and that column did not gain the rampart till half-past eleven.

Meanwhile, the lamented fall of Brigadier-General Gore and of Lieut. Colonel the Honourable George Carleton, and the dangerous wound of Major-General Skerrett, depriving the right column of their able direction, it fell into disorder, and suffered great loss in killed, wounded, and prisoners.

The centre column having been forced back with considerable loss by the heavy fire from the place (Lieut.-Colonel Morrice, its commander, and Lieut.-Colonel Elphinstone, commanding 33rd, being both wounded), was reformed under the command of Major Muttlebury 69th, marched round and joined Major General Cooke, the left wing of the 55th remaining to remove the wounded from the glacis.

However, the Guards, too, had suffered very severely during the night by the galling fire from the houses on their position, and by the loss of the detachment of the 1st Guards, which having been sent to endeavour to assist Lieut.-Colonel Carleton, and to secure the Antwerp gate, was cut off after the most gallant resistance, which cost the lives of many most valuable officers.

At daybreak, the enemy having turned the guns of the place opened their fire against the troops on the unprotected rampart, and the reserve of the 4th column (the Royal Scotch) retired from the Water-port gate, followed by the 33rd.

Major-General Cooke, then, despairing of success, directed the retreat of the Guards, which was conducted in the most orderly manner, protected by the remains of the right wing 55th and 69th Regiments (which corps repeatedly drove the enemy back with the bayonet), under the major-general's immediate direction.

The general afterwards found it impossible to withdraw these weak corps and having thus with the genuine feelings of a true soldier devoted himself, he surrendered to save the lives of the gallant men remaining with him.

I should wish to do justice to the great exertions and conspicuous gallantry of all those officers who had the opportunities of distinguishing themselves. I have not as yet been able to collect sufficient information.

Major-General Cooke reports to me his highest approbation generally of all the officers and men employed near him, particularly mentioning Colonel Lord Proby, Lieut.-Colonels Rooke, commanding the 3rd Guards, Mercer, commanding the light companies of the brigade (the latter unfortunately among the killed), Majors Muttlebury and Hogg, of the 69th and 55th, as deserving of his warm praise. He laments, in common with the whole corps, the severe loss to the service of those distinguished officers Lieut.-Colonel Clifton, commanding the 1st Guards, and Lieut.-Colonel the Honourable James Macdonald of that regiment. These officers fell, with many others, at the Antwerp gate, all behaving with the greatest intrepidity, and Lieut.-Colonel Jones with the remainder of the detachment was forced to surrender.

The service of conducting the columns was ably provided for by Lieutenant-Colonel C. Smyth, commanding Royal Engineers (he himself accompanied Major-General Cooke, as did also Lieut.-Colonel Sir G. Wood, commanding Royal Artillery), who attached officers to lead each column, *viz*: Captain Sir George Hoste and Lieutenant Abbey to the left, Lieutenant Sparling to the right, and Captain Edward Michell, Royal Artillery, who volunteered his services, to the centre columns, each having a party of sappers and miners under his command. Lieutenant Abbey was dangerously wounded, and Captain Michell was covered with wounds in the act of escalading the scarp-wall of the place, but I trust there are good hopes of his not being lost to the service.

Your Lordship will readily believe that though it is impossible not to feel the disappointment of ultimate failure in this attack, I can only think at present, with the deepest regret, of the loss of so many of my gallant comrades.

I have the honour, etc.,

Thos. Graham.

Private.

Headquarters, Calmthout,
20th March, 1814.

My Lord,

As I send Major Stanhope on purpose to enable your Lordship to know much more of the details of this unfortunate attack than I could possibly give in a letter, I need not enter into much explanation.

My chief inducement to undertake at last what I had all along resisted the temptation of, arose from three points of attack being satisfactorily explained by Dutch engineers well acquainted with the place, instead of one, and by the consideration of the increased importance of getting hold of such a barrier, should the events of the war in France bring the enemy back in force to this frontier.

It was necessary to carry into execution the plan almost as soon as it was determined on, to prevent the enemy from receiving information of the movements of the troops. It was not less so to watch Antwerp with increased vigilance. This prevented the concentration of as large a force as possible round Bergen-op-Zoom; but in truth, every account of the number and quality of the garrison led me to believe that if a footing could be gained on the rampart, success would be the result—there were near 4,000 men employed.

The garrison was stated to be reduced to less than 2,000—two thirds of the worst quality. In all this uniform information I have certainly been grossly deceived. There were 2,800 men who behaved well, though never standing for a moment a charge of our men, except where the numbers were greatly disproportionate. In short, the attack must have succeeded had the orders been obeyed. I enclose copies of them.

We had considerable reinforcements at hand soon after daylight from the 2nd Division, who, I had the mortification to find, arrived too late. Still, had the —— maintained the Water-port gate, General Cooke would have held his ground, and the place must have fallen.

But I will not trespass longer on your Lordship's patience in the details, which you will have more satisfactorily from Major Stanhope, on whose accuracy your Lordship may rely.

I have the honour, etc., etc.,

Thos. Graham.

To Lord Clancarty.

Calmthout, March 11th, 1814.

My Lord,

It has not been in my power sooner to give you an account of an attempt I made to gain possession of Bergen-op-Zoom but being anxious to put into your hands all the information on the subject which you may wish to lay before His Royal Highness the Prince of Orange, I send copies of the despatches I have sent home by Major Stanhope. I trust in all this His Royal Highness will see not only a proof of my zeal to be useful to the cause but will be satisfied that the enterprise must have been successful had the troops, particularly the right attack, not been sacrificed in small unsupported bodies—a misfortune which I endeavoured to prevent by the orders that were given to the different columns of attack.

I have the honour to be, etc.,

Thos. Graham.

To one so little accustomed to failure, this unsuccessful attempt was a severe blow, but considering that the troops employed were mostly recruits, that the assault was made in the dark, and that the orders, carefully framed and issued, were carelessly ignored, the most prejudiced must grant that General Graham had no cause to blame himself.

The intelligence furnished by persons within the fortress, supposed to be reliable, as to the strength and composition of the garrison, was quite sufficient to induce a man of General Graham's stamp to make an attempt to seize it. The information was incorrect, and although every precaution was taken to insure secrecy, still, as it afterwards became known, General Bizanet, the *commandant*, was aware at noon on the 8th that an attack was to be made. Success, therefore, would have been miraculous.

The answers to the plain unvarnished tale as contained in Sir Thomas Graham's despatch, prove that, however distasteful the news may have been, no one dreamt of attaching any blame to the commander of the British troops in Holland, whose conduct on the occasion was in after years described by one well able to judge, as composed of a "hardihood and daring which would alone place him amongst the foremost men of enterprise of which Europe can boast."

From the Duke of Clarence.

Hague, March 14th, 1814.

Dear Sir,

Yours of the 12th instant reached me last evening, and I have of course seen all the various papers you have sent to Lord Clancarty; I perfectly agree with you that the attack on Bergen-op-Zoom ought to have succeeded, as two of the columns got into the place. I regret the event on public grounds, but permit me to assure you I feel it most sensibly from private and personal attachment to yourself; your character was well known to me before I came to this country, but having been an eye-witness to your exertions and constant attention to the king's service, I entertain the highest sense of your merits, and knowing as I now do the different generals and commanding officers under your command, I feel singularly interested in the welfare and success of the gallant troops under your Excellency.

I am most anxiously looking for the Hanoverians, and in the event of being still here when you think you may recommence active operations, send me word, and I shall be happy and proud to be present at your capturing Bergen-op-Zoom, and completing the business at Antwerp.

God bless you, and ever believe me,

Dear Sir,

Yours unalterably,

William.

From Lord Clancarty.

The Hague, March 14th, 1814.

My dear Sir,

I received your despatch of the 12th last night, with the details of the late event at Bergen-op-Zoom, and very heartily condole with you upon results which neither from the nature of the information received concerning the strength and composition of the garrison, from the judgment with which the plan was laid, or the gallantry of the British troops, could reasonably have been apprehended.

However mournful the length of the list of casualties, or however much to be lamented the loss of such brave and skilful officers as are therein designated, it will be some consolation to the British Nation (and ought likewise to have this effect on you) to reflect that in neither of the latter there has been any failure; that if, whether in civil or military affairs, we are to act at all, we are all necessarily exposed to frequent and unavoidable deceit from misinformation; that, in the present instance, this could not have been avoided; that there is no enterprise of war which is not subject to mischance; that with respect to Bergen-op-Zoom, every reasonable probability existed of your success so as amply to warrant the risk, and the object shewn not to be the subject of a visionary plan from the very circumstances which attended the operation, of such magnitude not only to the cause of Holland, but to that of the allies, as fully to justify the hazard encountered for the purpose of its attainment. I have not a doubt that your conduct will be approved by our government, and however much I am sensible that your mind very poignantly feels the loss of the gallant fellows who have fallen on this occasion, and anxiety for those who have been wounded, you may rest assured that the fame which you have so loyally and bravely won will not be clouded by the recent failure.

Yours, my dear Sir,
Very sincerely,
Clancarty.
General Sir Thomas Graham, K.B.

From Lord Bathurst.
Downing Street, 15th March, 1814.
Sir,
I have had the honour of receiving your despatches, and I lost no time in laying them before the Prince Regent.

I have the satisfaction to say, that I am commanded by His Royal Highness to assure you that, however much he must regret the loss of so many brave officers and men, he is fully sensible of the daring spirit which dictated the enterprise, and the distinguished ability which, with a stricter attention to the directions given, would have ensured its success.

Had that success been complete, the exploit would have redounded to the honour of the British arms and would have largely contributed to the defence of Holland, should the fortune of war oblige the Allies to retreat from their present advanced position.

I have the honour to be, Sir,
    Your most obedient humble servant,

                                                        Bathurst.
General Sir Thomas Graham.

Major Stanhope, in his notes, mentions his visit as follows:—

> I waited on Lord Bathurst and was taken to Carlton House. Having explained to His Royal Highness the Prince Regent in detail everything that had passed, I concluded in expressing my hopes that his Royal Highness would not conceive that General Graham had wantonly thrown away the lives of his soldiers on a rash and impracticable plan, but that the attempt had been long considered, was well combined, and, as far as he was concerned, succeeded.
>
> The prince said, "So far, by God, from any blame being attached to Graham, I don't think he ever deserved more credit for any victory he ever gained, than for the combinations which ended in this failure."
>
> Lord Bathurst communicated to me afterwards from the prince, that he desired me to consider myself as a lieutenant-colonel, although it was perfectly unprecedented to give promotion for failure; but in this case he would give it to mark his peculiar approbation of Sir Thomas Graham's conduct.

From Lord Bathurst.

                            Downing Street, March 15th, 1814.

My dear General,

I hope my public despatch will be satisfactory to you. Major Stanhope will tell you how graciously he was received by the reent. As His Royal Highness "has been for some time confined, and is still very weak, I had at first a little difficulty in prevailing upon him to see Major Stanhope, particularly as His Royal Highness was just sitting down to his dinner; but I felt it to be of so much advantage that the case should be stated by the major, that I pressed it upon His Royal Highness, and I had the pleasure of seeing, not only that the account was completely satisfactory to the regent, but that it recommended the reporter in a particular manner to him.

As Major-General Taylor is fully instructed on every point I have to communicate to you, I have only to assure you that no one blames your conduct, and everyone admires your enterprising spirit.

I am,

Ever yours most sincerely,

Bathurst.

From Mr. Adam.

Lincoln's Inn, 15th March, 1814.

My dear Graham,

I wrote to you, as the date will shew, about Mrs. Maclaurin the day before the news of Bergen-op-Zoom. My son Francis, for a civilian, wrote a very good account of it, and of the causes of its misgiving, which will happen to the wisest and best-concerted plans. Still, your feelings must be different from those that accompany success.

You will, therefore, not think me officious, having the most anxious desire for your comfort as well as your glory, if I tell you what the Duke of York said to me yesterday, that the plan was most judicious, the measure well contrived for success, and the failure, however distressing, was the result of what you could neither have foreseen nor have counteracted.

Most affly and truly yours,

W. Adam.

From Lord Mulgrave.

March 22nd, 1814.

My dear Graham,

I saw Major Stanhope soon after his arrival (at the cabinet), and he fully convinced me of what I had before confidently anticipated, that your enterprise against Bergen-op-Zoom had been undertaken after cautious and measured deliberation, that the object was ascertained to be feasible, and that the best disposition had been made to secure success; in fact, as far as depended upon the general, the place was captured, and the subsequent reverses were what no providence could foresee and no vigilance avert, and what every night-operation must be liable to, even with the best troops, in a too-great eagerness for success; but where the instructions have not been followed by those entrusted with the execution, no responsibility can attach to the commander-in-chief. Regret, therefore, only attaches to the loss of the complete success of an enterprise, which, had it followed, would have secured an operation equally brilliant and important.

Ever yours most truly,

Mulgrave.

From Lieut.-Col. C. M. Cathcart to Viscount Cathcart, K.T.
(From Lord Cathcart's MSS.)

Headquarters of the British Army in Holland, Calmthout, April 1st, 1814.

My dearest Father,

I cannot sufficiently thank you for your most kind and affectionate letter of the 3rd *ult*,. which did not reach me until lately, having arrived in England just after I had left it for this country. I was perfectly satisfied with my situation in Lord Wellington's army, who was on all occasions particularly civil and kind to me, and on the most intimate and confidential terms with Sir Stapleton Cotton, with whom I lived. Never having heard from Sir Thomas Graham since he left that army I had not the least expectation of being called upon by him, particularly as an officer had been appointed to the only situation with him which could well be offered to me. However, on the morning of the 19th of January, whilst at breakfast, a courier arrived from headquarters with a letter from Lord Wellington.

The offer it contained, and the manner in which it was made was so flattering that I could not hesitate a moment in accepting it; I therefore mounted my horse and rode as fast as I could to headquarters and told Lord Wellington that I was fully sensible of his kindness, that I came to place myself at his disposal, and should be guided entirely by his advice and wishes. He said it was an offer I ought by all means to accept and should lose no time in embarking for England. I accordingly sailed from St. Sebastian on the 27th of January, but had a tedious passage, and did not reach England until the beginning of February.

On my arrival at the Horse Guards I found Torrens very much astonished to see me, and at the whole proceeding, for although aware that Sir Thomas was not satisfied with his quartermaster general, and wished one to be sent from Lord Wellington's army, he had not the slightest idea that they had gone so far, and that Lord Wellington himself had been written to. The marquis, being accustomed to prompt measures and to carry everything his own way, never doubted that other people could do the same, he therefore packed Mr. Dunmore, Deputy Commissary-General, and myself off, writing merely to say that he had sent us home at Sir Thomas Graham's request, to be at the head of our departments in Holland.

This, of course, caused considerable embarrassment and delay; reference was made to the general, who, when he found how far matters had gone, made a bold effort himself to complete the business by saying that if he was not to be allowed the privilege which almost every other officer going on command had enjoyed, *viz.*, that of choosing his own confidential staff, or at least of approving of their appointment, he should apply for leave to return home and quit the command altogether. This had the desired effect, and they were then as eager to get me away from London as they had been before to detain me. My predecessor behaved very well on the occasion, he is gone home on a month's leave, and is to return again to be an assistant under me.

I arrived, I believe, on the 3rd of March, the very day your letter was dated at this place, Sir Thomas Graham's headquarters. Our little corps has however, been engaged in no operations of any consequence, excepting the unfortunate attack on Bergen-op-Zoom, on the night of the 8th of March, the particulars of which you have of course seen long ago in the *Gazette*.

The attempt was certainly bold but is fully justified by the success which crowned the efforts of two of the columns of attack. In the first instance, they succeeded in surmounting every obstacle and establishing themselves on the ramparts; had the troops there been more experienced and better managed this important fortress must have been ours.

The information which induced the general to make this attack was very correct in every respect except with regard to the strength and quality of the garrison, which was represented as not exceeding 2,000 men, chiefly recruits and very old worn-out men; experience proved the contrary, as their numbers exceeded 3,000, and uncommon good troops. Notwithstanding the promptness with which the measure was carried into effect after it was determined upon—which was only about three o'clock the same morning—and the secrecy and caution with which the arrangements were made, the French governor afterwards informed us that he had received information of our intentions about noon that day, and was, of course, in some degree prepared.

I will not take up more of your time in recapitulating the details of this affair, but enclose a small sketch of the works, which is sufficient to show the different points by which the several columns were to enter.

The two that got into the place you may recollect were the guards, to the left of the Antwerp gate, and the column, commanded by General Skerrett, and led by Lieut.-Colonel Carlton, which forded at low water at the mouth of the haven, and entered by that means.

If the orders given previously had all been properly executed there was no reason why the centre attack near the Antwerp gate should not have succeeded also. The false attack commenced too soon, which placed the other troops under considerable disadvantages.

Sir Thomas is quite well and his eyes do not suffer much, although he uses, or rather abuses, them too much by writing night and day.

Believe me, my dearest Father,

  Ever your most affectionate Son,

C. M. C.

To the Viscount Cathcart.

Calmthout, 4th April.

I have but a moment, but I must take the opportunity of sending you two lines by Dawson, returning to Walmoden, to thank you for your two letters received last night from The Hague. You may imagine we shall be most impatient to hear of the great results which may be expected from the decisive movements on Paris. God grant they may be such as we all wish and hope. You are very kind in all you say about B.-op-Zoom; it ought to have been ours if the orders had been in any degree obeyed. The right column went on like a pack of fox-hounds into cover, and in all directions, and were annihilated before the guards got in,

It was a sad loss and disappointment, and for some time I could not muster philosophy enough to think of it without the deepest concern. You will see by the enclosed abstract what the intention was, and that is enough for your satisfaction. Everybody,

46

from the prince downward, at home has been kind beyond measure on the occasion, to a degree that I am almost ashamed of.

Adieu! we are heartily sick of this swampy country and wish ourselves further south. God bless you all.

Charles is quite fat, in perfect health, and a great comfort to me. Pray say everything kind to all my friends with you.

Ever affectionately yours,

Thos. Graham.

P.S.—I have mislaid the order and Charles is not in the way, but the 1st and 4th columns had positive orders to unite, the 1st by moving on the ramparts to its left, the 4th to its right, with that object, and then to move to assist the entry of the centre column and the opening of the Antwerp gate.

Captain Harris, Stewart's *A.D.C.*, passed with the news from Paris of the 30th.

From the Duke of Saxe Weimar.

Bruxelles, le 6 Avril, 1814.

Mon Général,

Reçevez mes sincères remercimens pour tout ce que vous avez la complaisance de faire pour nous. Le moment est très beau, et j'espère que nous sommes tous très pres du grand but.

J'ai l'honneur d'être, avec les sentimens d'une considération distinguée, De votre Excellence,

Le tout dévoué serviteur,

Charles Auguste.

Translation

Brussels, April 6th, 1814.

My general,

Receive my sincere thanks for all that you have the complacency to do for us. The moment is very beautiful, and I hope we are all very close to the big goal.

I have the honour to be, with the sentiments of distinguished consideration,

From your Excellency,

The devoted servant,

Charles Augustus.

About the middle of April, the British force in Holland was joined by the corps of the Duke of Brunswick, which, with that of General

Walmoden, was placed under the command of General Graham.

Before, however, any operations could be commenced the provisional Government in Paris proclaimed the fall of Napoleon and called upon the armies of France to give up the contest. The result of these proclamations was a suppression of hostilities in Holland, during which negotiations were entered into for the evacuation of the fortresses.

While occupied with these affairs, Sir Thomas Graham was informed that it was the intention of the prince regent to raise him to the peerage.

From Major-General Hope.

Horse Guards, April 29th, 1814.

My dear Graham,

I was yesterday called to London by Lord Melville and saw Lord Liverpool on my arrival.

His Lordship communicated to me an arrangement favoured by the regent for raising Lord Wellington to the rank of Duke, and to the Peerage

Sir J. Hope,

T. Graham,

Beresford,

Hill,

Cotton,

adding it was thus intended to mark to the army and the country how much their long course of honourable service had contributed to the glorious issue of the war.

Lord L. desired me to speak for my brother and you. Although fully possessed of your objections to a peerage, I considered this a case in which no individual feeling ought to prevail, as an exclusion from such a list would have hurt your name for ever. I, therefore, accepted for John and you, and have sought in the title of Lynedoch both to commemorate your military fame and, in private life, to keep alive a memorial of your pursuits and favourite improvements.

I shall write again in a few days, when I can address you by another title.

Your affectionate,

Alex. Hope.

Sir Thomas Graham, K. B.

Early in May Generals Carnot and Bizanet, commanding respectively at Antwerp and Bergen-op-Zoom, evacuated those fortresses, the former being occupied by the British, the latter by Dutch troops.

To Lord Bathurst.

Headquarters,
St. Gravenwesel, 3rd May, 1814.

My Lord,

I have the honour to inform your Lordship that Bergen-op-Zoom is to be occupied this day by the troops of the Dutch Army, under the command of His Royal Highness the Hereditary Prince of Orange, the French garrison retiring on Antwerp. The forts on the Scheldt were delivered up to us this morning. "On the 5th inst. the French garrison will be withdrawn from Antwerp, and the place will be occupied by British troops in the name of the allied sovereigns.

I have the honour, etc., etc.,

Thos. Graham.

Headquarters,
Antwerp, 5th May, 1814.

My Lord,

I have the honour to state to your Lordship that, agreeable to the terms of the convention of Paris of the 23rd *ult.*, this fortress, with the different forts depending on it, was finally evacuated by the remaining French troops this morning.

Major-General Künigl, the commissioner of the allied powers, having signified to me his wish that, according to his instructions, British troops should occupy it, the 1st Division, under the command of Major-General Cooke, with the 1st brigade of the 1st Division were marched in, and after the different guards were relieved, the new a garrison received the commissioner with military honours.

The magistrates then assembled on the parade and the mayor, recommending Antwerp to the protection, and its future fate to the favour of the allies, presented the keys of the town to General Künigl, who received them in the name of the allied sovereigns.

It is impossible to describe with what demonstrations of enthusiastic joy the inhabitants expressed their approbation of this interesting scene.

I have the honour to be, etc.,

Thos. Graham.

On the 3rd of May, General Graham was raised to the peerage by the style and title of Baron Lynedoch, of Balgowan, and a pension of £2,000 a year was granted him at the same time.

From Lord Mulgrave.

Harley Street, May 4th, 1814.

My dear Lord,

I cannot refrain from sending you a few words of congratulation on the high military honour which your manly perseverance has attained. No one of your numerous friends, either private or professional, can feel more truly rejoiced or more cordially gratified at the justice which has been done to your eminent services than I do.

Believe me, with great regard, ever yours most sincerely and faithfully,

Mulgrave.

To The Lord Lynedoch.

After the withdrawal of the French, Lord Lynedoch moved his headquarters to Brussels, where he received orders to assume the command of the whole of the allied forces in the Netherlands.

Bergen-op-Zoom, March 8-9, 1814

Colonel Percy Groves

After the defeat of the French at Leipzig, on the 16th and 18th of October, 1813, and the consequent advance of the allied armies towards the Rhine, the Emperor Napoleon found himself compelled to withdraw a considerable number of his troops from Holland and the Low Countries. Seizing this opportunity, the Dutch resolved to make an attempt to free themselves from the yoke of France; and on the 15th of November the inhabitants of Amsterdam rose *en masse*, with the cry of "*Orange Boven!*" hoisted the Orange flag, and proclaimed the *stadtholder*. The example of the Dutch capital was quickly followed by other towns, and in a few days the long-oppressed Hollanders were in open revolt.

On receiving intelligence of this rising, the British Government decided to afford material assistance to the Dutch, both in asserting their independence and in driving the remainder of the French troops from their country; so an expedition was organised, and several regiments received orders to hold themselves in readiness for immediate embarkation.

This expedition, which consisted of some 8,000 men, including three battalions of the Foot Guards, was placed under the command of General Sir Thomas Graham (afterwards Lord Lynedoch), who had just recovered from an illness, on account of which he had been invalided home from the Peninsula.

The Guards' Brigade sailed from Greenwich on the 24th of November, and, disembarking at Scheveling early in December, marched to The Hague. Having seen the Prince of Orange firmly re-established on his throne, the Guards proceeded to Willemstad, and on the 9th of January, 1814, they reached Steenbergen—which lies a few miles north of Bergen-op-Zoom—where Sir Thomas Graham was enabled to effect a junction with the allied troops cantoned on his left at Oudenbosch and Breda.

The weather at this time was very inclement, and the British soldiers suffered severely from the bitter cold.

Early in January, 1814, the French had assembled all their available forces at Antwerp, and, after various movements, Sir Thomas Graham, in concert with the Prussian general, Bülow, made an attack, on the 2nd of February, on Merxem, with the object of moving against Antwerp. The village of Braachstad was quickly captured, and next day batteries were erected and fire opened; but, unfortunately, the mortars and ammunition, which had been brought from Willemstad, proved so defective that after three days the troops returned to their cantonments. The investment of Antwerp was, however, continued.

While investing Antwerp, General Graham conceived a scheme for carrying, by a *coup de main*, the important fortress-town of Bergen-op-Zoom, which was held by a strong French garrison.

Bergen-op-Zoom, a fortified town of old Dutch Brabant, is situated on the right bank of the Scheldt, and derives its name from the little River Zoom, which, after supplying the defences with water, discharges itself into the Scheldt. It lies some five leagues north of Antwerp, and seven south-west of Breda. The old channel of the Zoom, into which the tide flows towards the centre of the town, forms the harbour, and is nearly dry at low water. There were four principal entrances into the town—three by land, through the Steenbergen Gate in the north face of the fortifications, the Antwerp Gate in the south face, and the New Gate in the east face; and one by a canal—which communicated with the River Scheldt, and, in fact, formed a part of the harbour—through the Waterport Gate, in the west face. The fortress was garrisoned by 5,000 or 6,000 French troops, under command of General Bizonet, a very able officer.

Sir Thomas Graham and his colleagues calculated that the severe frost would prevent the sluices from being used to raise or lower the water, and that the ice in the ditches of the fortress would only be partially broken; so Sir Thomas determined to carry into execution his plan, which was certainly a daring one, and well considered.

Graham's command had recently received reinforcements—including a strong draft for the Guards' Brigade; the 4th Battalion 1st Royal Scots, which had marched from the north of Germany, and was cantoned at Rosendal; and the 2nd Battalion Royal North British Fusiliers, stationed at Tholen.

Having decided on the attack, Sir Thomas lost no time in making the necessary arrangements, and on the 8th of March 4,000 troops were detached from the army investing Antwerp, and marched secretly to the neighbourhood of Bergen-op-Zoom. This force was told off into four "columns of attack," as follows:—

1st Column.—Detachments of the Guards' Brigade (1,000), under Colonel Lord Proby, 2nd Battalion 1st Foot Guards.

2nd Column.—33rd (600), 55th (250), and 2nd Battalion 69th Foot (350), under Lieutenant-Colonel Morice, 69th Foot.

★★★★★★

The 2nd Battalion 69th Foot.—This battalion was raised in 1803, and disbanded in 1816 or 1817. The 69th was subsequently known as the 2nd Battalion the Welsh Regiment.— The 2nd Battalion 21st Royal North British Fusiliers (subsequently Royal Scots Fusiliers), raised in Ayrshire in 1804, and disbanded in 1816.—The 2nd Battalion 91st Foot, raised in 1804 and disbanded in 1816. The 91st (raised as the 98th) subsequently styled the "1st Battalion Princess Louise's Argyll and Sutherland Highlanders." The 2nd Battalion 37th Foot (now "1st Battalion Hampshire Regiment"), raised in 1811 and disbanded in 1815-16.—The 4th Battalion 1st Foot, or "Royal Scots," embodied at Hamilton, North Britain, on Christmas Day, 1804, and disbanded at Dover on the 24th of March, 1816. This ancient regiment, which traces its origin to the Scots Guards in the service of the king of France in 882, was in 1684 styled the "Royal Regiment of Foot," and some years later was numbered the 1st of the British Line. In 1812 it was styled the 1st or "Royal Scots," and in 1821 the "Royal Regiment." The designation "Royal Scots" was restored to the regiment in 1871, and subsequently known as the "Royal Scots (Lothian Regiment)."—The 2nd Battalion 44th Foot, raised in Ireland in 1803-4, and disbanded at Dover early in 1816. The 44th was subsequently known as the "1st Battalion the Essex Regiment."

★★★★★★

3rd Column.—2nd Battalion 21st Fusiliers (100), 37th (150), and 2nd Battalion 91st Foot (400), under Brevet Lieutenant-Colonel Henry, 21st Fusiliers.

4th Column.—Flank Companies of the 21st and 37th (200), 4th Battalion Royal Scots (600), and 2nd Battalion 44th Foot (300), under Brigadier-General Gore and Lieutenant-Colonel the Honourable G.

Carleton, accompanied by Major-General Skerrett.

Major-General George Cooke was in supreme command.

The 1st column, led by Cooke, formed the left of the line, and was destined to attack the works between the Waterport and Antwerp Gates. The 2nd column was to attack the right of the New Gate; while the 3rd column made a feint on the Steenbergen Gate, to call off the attention of the enemy from the more serious attacks, and to be disposable according to circumstances. The 4th—or right—column, accompanied by the gallant Skerrett—the former temporary Brigadier of the Guards in the Peninsula—was to force the entrance of the harbour, which was fordable at low water.

A detachment of the Royal Sappers and Miners—about forty men in all—provided with axes, saws, crowbars, and a few scaling-ladders, was distributed between the four columns.

As soon as the 1st (Guards) and 4th columns gained an entrance to the fortress, they were to push along the ramparts, and, having effected a junction, proceed to clear them of the enemy and assist the other attacks.

Such was the general plan of attack: we shall now see how it was carried out.

The hour for the assault was fixed for 10.30 on the night of the 8th of March, and at that hour the four columns advanced.

We will first follow the movements of the 4th column, of which the following graphic account is given by a subaltern officer of the 21st Fusiliers, who, having missed his own regiment, attached himself to the Royal Scots, and thereby came in for the very hottest of the fighting. This young officer in the *United Service Journal* for 1830 writes:—

We had all become thoroughly sick of the monotony of our duties at Tholen, when we received orders to march the next day (the 8th March, 1814). As the attack on Bergen-op-Zoom which took place that evening was, of course, kept a profound secret, the common opinion was that we were destined for Antwerp, where the other division of the army had already had some fighting.

It was nearly dark when we arrived at the village of Halsteren, which is only three or four miles from Bergen-op-Zoom, where we took up our quarters for the night. On the distribution of billets to the officers, I received one upon a farmhouse about a mile in the country, where I was presently joined by four or five officers of the 4th Battalion Royal Scots, who told me that they believed an attempt to surprise Bergen-op-Zoom would be made that night.

Learning from my new acquaintances that the grenadier company of their battalion, which was commanded by an old friend of mine (Lieutenant Allan Robertson) whom I had not seen for some years, was only about a mile further off, I thought I should have time to see him and join my regiment before they marched, should they be sent to the attack. However, the party of the Royal Scots whom I accompanied lost their way from their ignorance of the road, and we in consequence made a long circuit, during which I heard from an *aide-de-camp*, who passed us, that the 21st were on their march to attack the place in another quarter from us.

In these circumstances I was exceedingly puzzled what course to take: if I went in search of my regiment, I had every chance of missing them in the night, being quite ignorant of the roads. Knowing that the Royal Scots would be likely to head one of the assaulting columns, from the number of the regiment, I took what I thought to be the surest plan, by attaching myself to the grenadier company of the Royal Scots under my gallant friend.

After mustering the men, we marched to the general *rendezvous* of the regiments forming the 4th column: the Royal Scots led the column, followed by the other regiments according to their number. As everything depended on our taking the enemy by surprise, the strictest orders were given to observe a profound silence on the march.

When we had proceeded some way we fell in with a picket, commanded by Captain Darrah, of the 21st Fusiliers, who was mustering his men to proceed to the attack. Thinking that our regiment must pass his post on their way to the false attack, he told me to remain with him until they came up. I, in consequence, waited some time, but, hearing nothing of the regiment and losing patience, I gave him the slip in the dark, and ran on until I regained my place with the grenadier company of the Royal Scots. (Selections from the very useful account provided by this officer appear throughout Colonel Groves' article. It also appears in full within this book and readers are asked to

"WE GOT INTO SOME CONFUSION IN LABOURING THROUGH THIS HORRIBLE
SLOUGH"

bear with the element of repetition in the interests of cohesion within the text—Leonaur Editors.)

On nearing the point of attack, the column crossed the Tholen-dike, and entered the bed of the Zoom, through which our troops had to make their way before reaching the wet ditch. It was terrible work pushing through the thick deep mud of the river: the men sank nearly to their waists, and as they advanced, fell into some confusion—the various companies getting mixed up. Many poor fellows were trodden down and smothered in the mud, but the more fortunate pressed on, and a considerable portion of the column succeeded in passing through this veritable "Slough of Despond," and entered the ditch.

So far the French garrison had not taken alarm, but now some thoughtless men raised a cheer, probably to encourage their comrades. General Skerrett, who was at the head of the column, was furious with rage, and passed word to the rear for strict silence to be observed. Unfortunately, the mischief was done: that one cheer had alarmed the garrison, who at once opened the sluices and sent a torrent of water down upon their assailants, while almost at the same moment a brilliant firework was displayed upon the ramparts, showing up every object as clear as if it were daylight.

In spite of this, General Skerrett, with a good number of his men, cleared the bed of the river, and gained the ditch. The Fusilier officer continues:—

The point at which we entered was a bastion to the right of the harbour, from one of the angles of which a row of high palisades was carried through the ditch. To enable us to pass the water, some scaling-ladders had been sunk to support us in proceeding along the palisades, over which we had to climb with each other's assistance. So great were the obstacles we met with, that had not the attention of the enemy fortunately (or rather most judiciously) been distracted by the false attack under Lieut.-Col. Henry it appeared quite impossible for us to have effected an entrance at this point.

While we were proceeding forward in this manner, Colonel Muller of the Royal Scots was clambering along the tops of the palisades, calling to those who had got the start of him to endeavour to open the Waterport Gate and let down the drawbridge to our right; but no one, in the hurry of the moment, seemed to hear him. On getting near enough, I told him

I should effect it, if it was possible.

We met with but trifling resistance on gaining the rampart: the enemy being panic struck, fled to the streets and houses in the town, from which they kept up a pretty smart fire upon us for some time. I got about twenty soldiers of different regiments to follow me to the Waterport Gate, which we found closed. It was constructed of thin paling, with an iron bar across it about three inches in breadth. Being without tools of any kind, we made several ineffectual attempts to open the gate: at last, retiring a few paces, we made a rush at it in a body, when the iron bar snapped in the middle like a bit of glass. Some of my people got killed and wounded during this part of the work, but when we got to the drawbridge we were a little more sheltered from the firing.

The bridge was up, and secured by a lock in the right-hand post of the two which supported it. I was simple enough to attempt to pick the lock with a bayonet, but after breaking two or three, we at last had an axe brought us from the bastion, where our troops were entering. With this axe we soon succeeded in cutting the lock out of the post, and, taking hold of the chain, I had the satisfaction to pull down the drawbridge with my own hands.

While I was engaged in this business Colonel Muller was forming the Royal Scots on the rampart where we entered; but a party of about one hundred and fifty men of different regiments, under General Skerrett—who must have entered to the left of the harbour—was clearing the ramparts towards the Steenbergen Gate, where the false attack had been made by the 3rd column under Lieut.-Col. Henry; while another party, under Colonel Carleton of the 44th Regiment, was proceeding in the opposite direction along the ramparts to the right, without meeting with much resistance.

Hearing the firing on the opposite side of the town from General Skerrett's party, and supposing that they had marched through the town, I ran on through the streets to overtake them, accompanied by only one or two men; for the rest had left me and returned to the bastion after we had opened the gate. In proceeding along the canal or harbour which divided this part of the town I came to a loopholed wall, which was continued from the houses down to the water's edge. I observed a party

"WE SOON SUCCEEDED IN CUTTING THE LOCK OUT OF THE
POST"

of soldiers within a gate in this wall, and was going up to them, taking them for our own people, when I was challenged in French, and had two or three shots fired at me.

Seeing no other way of crossing the harbour but by a little bridge which was nearly in a line with the wall, I returned to the Waterport Gate which I found Colonel Muller had taken possession of with two or three companies of his regiment. I went up to him, and told him that I had opened the gate according to his desire, and also informed him of the interruption I had met with in the town, and he sent one of his companies up with me to the wall already mentioned, ordering the officer in command of the company to drive the enemy away, and hold the wall and gate until further orders.

On coming to the gate we met with a sharp resistance, but, after firing a few rounds and preparing to charge, the Frenchmen gave way, leaving us in possession of the gate and bridge. Leaving the company here, and crossing the little bridge, I again set forward alone to overtake General Skerrett's party, guided by the firing on the ramparts. Avoiding any little parties of the enemy, I had reached the inside of the ramparts where the firing was, without its occurring to me that I might get into the wrong box and be taken prisoner. Fortunately, I observed a woman looking over a shop door on one side of the street. I asked her where the British soldiers were, and she told me without hesitation, pointing at the same time in the direction. I shook hands with her, and bade her 'goodnight,' not entertaining the smallest suspicion of her deceiving me; and, following her directions, I clambered up the inside of the rampart and joined General Skerrett's party.

The moon had now risen, and though the sky was cloudy we could see pretty well what was doing. Here I found my friend Robertson, with the grenadier company of the Royal Scots, and I learned from him that the party—which was now commanded by Captain Guthrie, of the 33rd Regiment—had been compelled by numbers to retire from the bastion, which the enemy now occupied; and that Guthrie intended to endeavour to hold the one he was now in possession of, until he could procure a reinforcement. Robertson also told me that General Skerrett had been dangerously wounded, and taken prisoner, which was an irreparable loss to our party, as Captain Guthrie was ignorant of the general's intentions.

In the meantime the enemy kept up a sharp fire on us, which we returned as fast as our men could load their firelocks. Several of the enemy who had fallen, as well as of our own men, were lying on the ramparts. We presently discovered a large pile of logs of wood on the ramparts, and these we quickly disposed across the gorge of the bastion, so as to form a kind of parapet over which our people could fire, leaving, however, about half the distance open towards the parapet of the rampart. On the opposite side of the bastion were two 24-pounders, raised on high platforms, and these guns we turned on the enemy, firing along the ramparts over the heads of our own party. But, however valuable this resource might be to us, we were still far from being on equal terms with the French, who, besides greatly exceeding us in numbers, had brought up two or three field-pieces, which annoyed us much during the night. There was also a windmill on the bastion the Frenchmen occupied, from the top of which their musketry did great execution among us. In the course of the night the enemy made several ineffectual attempts to drive us from our position; but on these occasions—of which we were always made aware by the shouts they raised to encourage each other—as soon as they made their appearance on the rampart, we gave them a good dose of grape from our 24-pounders, and had a party ready to charge them back. I observed our soldiers were always disposed to meet the enemy halfway, and the latter were soon so well aware of our humour, that they invariably turned tail before we could get within forty or fifty paces of them.

The firing was kept up almost continually on both sides until about two o'clock in the morning, when it would sometimes cease for more than half-an-hour together. During one of these intervals of stillness, being exhausted with our exertions and the cold we felt in our drenched clothes, some of us lay down along the parapet together, in hopes of borrowing a little heat from each other, and presently fell into a troubled, dozing state, when I suddenly felt the ground shake under me, and heard at the same time a crash as if the whole town had been overwhelmed by an earthquake; a bright glare of light burst on my eyes at the same instant, and almost blinded me.

A shot from the enemy had blown up our small magazine on

the ramparts, on which we depended for the supply of the two 24-pounders which had been of such material use to us during the night. This broke our slumbers most effectually, and we had now nothing for it but to maintain our ground in the best way we could, until we received a reinforcement from some of the other parties.

Immediately after this disaster the enemy, raising a tremendous shout, or rather yell, attempted to come to close quarters with us, in hopes of our being utterly disheartened; but our charging party, which we had always in readiness, made them wheel round as usual. In the course of the night we had sent several small parties of men to represent the state of our detachment and endeavour to procure assistance; but none of them returned, having, we supposed, been intercepted by the enemy. Discouraged though we were by this circumstance, we still continued to hold our ground until the break of day.

While the events described in the above narrative were taking place, the main portion of the 4th column had also met with disaster: after all their toil and gallantry, the Royal Scots and their comrades of the 33rd—which regiment had been sent to reinforce Colonel Muller during the night—saw the prize which they had gained at such frightful cost snatched from their grasp.

We have already seen how Colonel Muller, with the battalion companies of the Royal Scots, took possession of the ramparts round the Waterport Gate. Before very long the battalion found itself exposed to a murderous grape and musketry fire from a couple of howitzers, and a small detachment of French marines stationed in the vicinity of the arsenal. Colonel Muller at once detached two companies to keep the enemy in check, and these detached companies—which were relieved every two hours—were actively engaged in this arduous service from 11 p.m. until daybreak, when the enemy made a furious attack in strong columns which bore down all before them.

The detached companies were now quickly driven in by overwhelming numbers, while the battalion, being exposed to a terrible fire from the guns of the arsenal, was forced to retire by the Waterport Gate, only to receive the fire of a detached battery. Finding himself thus placed between two fires, with a high palisade on one hand and the Zoom filled with tide on the other, Colonel Muller preferred to surrender rather than throw away the lives of his soldiers. The colours of the battalion were first sunk in the River Zoom by Lieutenant and Adjutant Galbraith; the battalion then surrendered, on condition that the officers and men should not serve against the French until exchanged, and on the following day it marched out of Bergen-op-Zoom "with all the honours of war."

In this disastrous affair the 4th Battalion Royal Scots lost 4 officers and 37 non-commissioned officers and men killed; 4 officers and 71 non-commissioned officers and men wounded.

The 33rd also suffered severe losses.

We left the small party, under Captain Guthrie of the 33rd, holding the position they had so gallantly won, and hoping against hope that, sooner or later, they would be relieved from the terrible predicament in which they found themselves; but the first dawn of day plainly showed the devoted men the utter hopelessness of their situation. By this time the firing had entirely ceased in other parts of Bergen-op-Zoom, and so, in absence of all communication, Guthrie and his comrades could only believe that the British troops had been driven from the place, and that there was nothing for them but to surrender, or die where they stood. The former alternative, however, does not appear to have entered their minds.

The French now brought an overwhelming force against them, but they still hoped, from the narrowness of the rampart, to be able to hold their own. In this they were deceived. The bastion was extensive, but only that portion of it near the gorge was furnished with a parapet. At this spot, and behind the logs which Guthrie and his men had piled up, the now greatly diminished party was collected. Keeping up a hot fire, in order to divert attention, the French detached part of their force, which, skirting the outside of the ramparts, and ascending the face of the bastion occupied by Guthrie, suddenly opened a murderous fire on his left flank and rear. From this fire Guthrie's men were entirely unprotected, while the French were sheltered by the top of the rampart. Lieutenant —— continues:—

The slaughter was now dreadful, and our poor fellows, who had done all that soldiers could do in our trying situation, fell thick and fast. Just at this time my friend Robertson, under whose command I had put myself at the beginning of the attack, fell. I had just time to run up to him, and found him stunned from a wound in the head, when our gallant commander, seeing the inutility of continuing the unequal contest, gave the order to retreat.

We had retired in good order about three hundred yards when poor Guthrie received a wound in the head, which I have since been informed deprived him of his sight. The enemy, when they saw us retreating, hung upon our rear, keeping up a sharp fire all the time, but they still seemed to have some respect for us from the trouble we had already given them. We had indulged the hope that, by continuing our course along the ramparts, we should be able to effect our retreat by the Waterport Gate, not being aware that we should be intercepted by the mouth of the harbour, and we were already at the very margin before we discovered our mistake and found ourselves completely hemmed in by the French; so there was no alternative left to us but to surrender as prisoners of war, or to attempt to escape across the harbour by means of the floating pieces of ice with which the water was covered.

Not one of us seemed to entertain the idea of surrender, and in the despair which had now taken possession of every heart we threw ourselves into the water, or leaped for the broken pieces of ice which were floating about.

The scene that ensued was shocking beyond description! The canal, or harbour, was faced on both sides by high brick walls, and in the middle of the channel lay a small Dutch vessel, which was secured by a rope to the opposite side of the harbour. Our only hope of preserving our lives, or effecting our escape, depended on our being able to gain this little vessel. Already many had, by leaping first on one piece of ice and then on another, succeeded in getting on board the vessel, which they hauled, by means of the rope, to the opposite side of the canal, and thus freed our obstruction; but, immediately afterwards being intercepted by the Waterport redoubt, they were compelled to surrender. Among the rest, I had scrambled down the face of the canal to a beam, running horizontally along the brick-work, from which other beams descended perpendicularly into the water, to prevent the sides being injured by the shipping. After sticking my sword into my belt (for I had thrown the scabbard away the previous night), I leaped from this beam—which was nine or ten feet above the water—for a piece of ice, but, not judging my distance very well, it tilted up with me, and I sank to the bottom of the canal.

"SEVERAL MEN WERE STILL HANGING ON TO OTHER PIECES OF ICE"

However, I soon came up again, and after swimming to the other side of the canal, and to the vessel, and finding nothing to catch hold of, I returned to the piece of ice upon which I had first leapt, and, swinging my body under it, managed to keep my face above water. I was not the only survivor of those who had got into the water: several men were still hanging on to other pieces of ice, but one by one they let go their hold and sank as their strength failed, until only three or four, besides myself, remained. All this time some of the enemy continued firing at us, and I saw one or two poor fellows shot in the water near me.

So intent was everyone on effecting his escape, that though they sometimes cast a look of commiseration at their drowning comrades, no one thought for a moment of giving us any assistance. The very hope of it had at length so completely faded in our minds that we ceased to ask the aid of those who floated past us upon fragments of ice; but Providence had reserved one individual who possessed a heart to feel for the distress of his fellow-creatures more than for his own personal safety. The very last person who reached the Dutch vessel was Lieut. McDougal of the 91st Regiment, and by his assistance I, too, succeeded in getting on board.

While assisting McDougal to save two or three soldiers who still clung to pieces of ice, I received a musket-ball through my wrist; for the enemy continued deliberately firing at us from the opposite rampart, which was not above sixty yards from the vessel. After this I went down to the cabin, where I found Lieut. Briggs of the 91st sitting on one side with a severe wound through his shoulder-blade.

★★★★★★

Lieutenant James Briggs, 91st (afterwards Major Sir James Briggs, K.H.) exchanged to the 63rd Foot, and retired in 1837. He was reported killed.

★★★★★★

The floor of the cabin was covered with water, for the vessel had become leaky from the firing. I managed to bind up my wounded wrist with my neckcloth so as in some measure to stop the bleeding, and we remained, cold and miserable, in the cabin for several hours. During that time the water continued to rise higher and higher, until it reached my middle.

Fortunately, the vessel grounded from the receding of the tide, and, escape in our condition being now quite out of the question, my companion and I were glad, on the whole, to be relieved from our truly disagreeable position by surrendering ourselves prisoners of war.

★★★★★★

The officer who wrote the above narrative was taken to a hospital in the town, where his wounds were dressed. He was subsequently released, and rejoined the 2nd Battalion 21st Fusiliers at Wouw. We cannot, with any certainty, identify this officer; but as only two subalterns of the 21st appear in the casualty list as wounded and taken prisoners at Bergen-op-Zoom, he must have been one of the two—namely, 2nd Lieut. J. W. Dunbar Moody, or 2nd Lieut. David Rankine. The 21st lost nine officers killed, wounded and missing, including Brevet Lieut.-Col. Henry, who commanded the 3rd column.

★★★★★★

Having described the disasters which befell the 4th column, we will now turn to the movements of the 1st, 2nd, and 3rd columns, whose efforts, unfortunately, met with no better success.

The 1st, or Guards, column, under Colonel Lord Proby, was, as we have already stated, destined to attack the works between the Waterport and Antwerp Gates. Between the point of attack and the Antwerp Gate the enemy had a strongly entrenched camp. At the appointed hour the Guardsmen, accompanied by Major-General Cooke, advanced from the Antwerp road, and, skirting the salient of the *lunette* of the entrenched camp, they reached the broad wet ditch of the unrevetted fronts (between the Waterport Gate and the *lunette*) without being discovered by the enemy. So far all had gone well; but now it was found that, owing to the rise and fall of the tide, the ice at the point where the ditch was to have been crossed was not sufficiently thick to stand the passage of the column. Lord Proby at once reported this untoward circumstance to General Cooke, who ordered him to move his men more to the right, towards the ditch of the "Orange Bastion," where a *batardeau*, preventing the action of the tide, allowed the ice to form strong enough to support them.

This spot reached, the advanced and ladder parties of the Guards, under Captain Rodney and Ensigns Gooch and Pardoe, quickly crossed the frozen ditch, followed by the rest of the column. Under the direction of Lieutenant-Colonel Smyth, R.E., and Captain Sir G.

Hoste, the ladders were placed against the *demi-revetment* (seventeen feet high), and the Guardsmen, swarming up, gained possession of the ramparts without meeting with much opposition beyond a slight musketry fire from the flanks. Major-General Cooke, with the officers commanding Royal Artillery and Engineers, entered the place with the Guards.

Owing to the delay caused by the unavoidable change in the point of attack, it was 11.30 p.m. before the 1st column established itself on the ramparts of Bergen-op-Zoom.

Though surprised by the first assault, the French garrison was not thrown into confusion, and was soon again in a position to resist the British troops.

Suspecting from the quiet that reigned at the French posts opposite the other intended points of attack that the several columns had not yet entered, Cooke formed the Guards on the ramparts in column of sections, and also occupied some houses in front, and in the adjoining bastion, from which his men might otherwise have been seriously annoyed. The ladders by which the Guards had entered were left standing against the scarp, so that a ready communication with the exterior was ensured.

A strong patrol was now despatched to the left, towards the Waterport Gate, to ascertain whether the 4th column had entered; and a detachment of the 1st Foot Guards, under Lieut.-Col. Clifton, was sent along the ramparts to the right, with orders to secure the Antwerp Gate, and to support, or at least gain some intelligence of, the 2nd column under Lieut.-Col. Morrice. General Cooke in his despatch of the 10th March, 1814, writes:—

> Lieut.-Col. Clifton reached the Antwerp Gate, but found that it could not be opened by his men, the enemy throwing a very heavy fire upon a street leading to it. It was also found that they occupied an outwork commanding the bridge, which would effectually render that outlet useless to us. I heard nothing more of this detachment, but considered it as lost, the communication having been interrupted by the enemy. Lieut.-Col. Rooke, with a party of the 2nd Foot Guards, was afterwards sent in that direction, and driving the enemy from the intermediate rampart, reached the Antwerp Gate; but he found it useless to attempt anything, and ascertained that the outwork was still occupied.

Rooke was thus compelled to rejoin the main body of the column, after his party had been pretty severely handled, without having gleaned any tidings of the missing detachment, whose fate, as we shall see, was learned later on.

After making a most gallant charge on the enemy, and capturing a field-piece at the point of the bayonet. Colonel Clifton and his men had found themselves cut off by a very superior force. The Guardsmen offered a most determined resistance, but being exposed to a destructive fire on all sides, which placed many officers (including Clifton himself) and men *hors de combat,* they were at length obliged to surrender. Amongst the officers taken prisoner was Lieut.-Col. Jones, upon whom the command of the ill-fated detachment devolved after the gallant Clifton's fall.

While the Guards were engaged in their attack the 2nd column had made an unsuccessful attempt on the works to the right of the New Gate, in which it lost upwards of 200 men killed and wounded, including its leader, Lieut.-Col. Morrice, and Lieut.-Col. Elphinstone, of the 33rd Foot.

The 33rd, 55th, and 69th were driven back in some confusion, but they quickly re-formed, and, leaving the left wing of the 55th to remove their wounded, they moved off to the support of the 1st column. It will be remembered that the scaling-ladders used by the 1st column had been left in position, and by this means the men of the 33rd, 55th, and 69th gained the summit of the ramparts, joined the 1st column, and were formed up to the left of the Guards, who still held their position, though they had for hours been exposed to a galling fire from those houses which still remained in possession of the enemy.

Though thus reinforced. General Cooke—who was still uncertain as to how matters were going on in other quarters of the town—did not think it expedient to make any further attempts to carry points which he might not be able to maintain, or to expose his troops to certain loss by penetrating through the streets; but on receiving intelligence that Colonel Muller was holding the Waterport Gate against heavy odds, he sent the 33rd to his assistance.

Throughout that long night the French garrison kept up a hot fire upon General Cooke's position, and at one time they held an adjoining bastion, from the angle of which they completely commanded his communication with the exterior. They were, however, charged, and driven away from this point of vantage in a very spirited style by the 55th and 69th, under Majors Hogg and Muttlebury.

At length, finding that matters were becoming serious, and being still without any certain information from other quarters, General Cooke determined, at the suggestion of Lord Proby, to let part of the Foot Guards withdraw, which was done by means of the ladders at the point where they entered. At daybreak, the enemy again possessed themselves of the bastion commanding the communications, from which they were again driven by Hogg and Muttlebury with their weak battalions. About 6 a.m. the enemy directed their first attack in force upon the British troops holding the Waterport Gate, and General Cooke had now the mortification of witnessing the Royal Scots and the 33rd retire from that position without being able to render them any assistance. At the same time the French gunners opened a heavy cannonade upon the Guards and the 55th and 69th, who still remained on the open ramparts.

Seeing that all was lost. General Cooke ordered the rest of the Guards to retire. The retreat was conducted in the most orderly manner, covered by the 69th and 55th; the latter corps, led by the general in person, repeatedly driving the enemy back. These weak battalions as they crossed the ditch were so much exposed to an incessant concentrated fire of musketry and artillery, that the general saw it would be impossible to withdraw them; and he was contemplating a surrender, when Lieut.-Col. Jones, of the 1st Foot Guards—who had been taken prisoner after the destruction of Clifton's detachment—arrived on the scene, accompanied by a French officer, with a flag of truce. Cooke, in his despatch says:—

Lieut.-Col. Jones informed me that Lieut.-Col. Muller and the troops at the Waterport Gate had been obliged to surrender, and were marched prisoners into the town. I now also learnt the fate of Lieut.-Col. Clifton's detachment and of Major-Generals Skerrett and Gore and Lieut.-Col. Carleton (Major-General Skerrett was dangerously wounded; Brigadier-General Gore, of the 33rd, and Lieut.-Col. the Hon. G. Carleton, of the 44th, were killed); and that the troops who had followed them had suffered very much, and had been repulsed from the advanced points along the ramparts, where they had penetrated to. I was now convinced that a longer continuance of the contest would be a useless loss of lives, and I therefore consented to adopt the mortifying alternative of laying down our arms.

It is strange that no mention is made in the despatches of either

Generals Graham or Cooke of the movements of the 3rd column, and we can find no details of the part it played in the attack—beyond the fact that it made a feint on the Steenbergen Gate. Whether Lieut.-Col. Henry turned this false attack into a real one, or whether he joined the 4th column, we cannot say for certain; but it is evident that the 3rd column entered Bergen-op-Zoom, and was hotly engaged, for Lieut.-Col. Henry and his second-in-command, Lieut.-Col. Ottley, were both wounded, and the corps (21st, 37th, and 91st), composing the column, suffered heavy losses.

The total loss of the British in this disastrous affair was about 300 killed and 1,800 prisoners, many of the latter being wounded.

★★★★★★

Thus ended the memorable attack upon Bergen-op-Zoom, in which, though defeated, the troops engaged were not disgraced. The failure of the enterprise was due, in a great measure, to circumstances over which General Cooke had no control: unforeseen difficulties cropped up which would have tended to frustrate the very best concerted plan of operations; and however much the disastrous termination was deplored, it was freely acknowledged that there had been few occasions during the long war with France in which the courage and energies of British soldiers were put to a more severe test, or were met by a more gallant and successful resistance on the part of the enemy.

BERGEN-OP-ZOOM.

The Full Eyewitness Account of the Attack on Bergen-op-Zoom by Lieutenant J. W. Dunbar Moodie, (21st Fusiliers)

There are certain events in the life of every man on which the memory dwells with peculiar pleasure; and the impressions they leave, from being interwoven with, his earliest and most agreeable associations, are not easily effaced from his mind. Sixteen years have now elapsed since the short campaign in Holland, and the ill-fated attack on Bergen-op-Zoom; but almost every circumstance that passed under my notice at that period, still remains as vividly pictured in my mind as if it had occurred but yesterday.

Our regiment, the 21st, or Royal North British Fusiliers, was stationed at Fort George when the order came for our embarkation for Holland. Whoever has experienced the dull monotony of garrison duty, may easily conceive the joy with which the intelligence was hailed. The eve of our embarkation was spent in all the hilarity inspired by the occasion, and, as may be supposed, the bottle circulated with more than ordinary rapidity. Our convoy, Captain Nixon, R.N. in return for some kindness he had met with from my family, while on the Orkney station, insisted on my taking my passage to Helvoet Sluys, along with our commanding officer and acting-adjutant, on board his own vessel, the *Nightingale*.

The scene that was exhibited next day, as we were embarking, must be familiar to most military men. The beach presented a spectacle I shall never forget. While the boats, crowded with soldiers, with their arms glittering in the sun, were pushing off, women were to be seen up to their middles in the water, bidding, perhaps, a last farewell to

THE ATTACK ON BERGEN-OF-ZOOM.

their husbands; while others were sitting disconsolate on the rocks, stupefied with grief, and almost insensible of what was going forward. Many of the poor creatures were pouring out blessings on the officers and begging us to be kind to their husbands. At last, when we had got the soldiers fairly seated in their places, which was no easy task, we pulled off, while the shouts of our men were echoed back in wailings and lamentations, mixed with benedictions, from the unhappy women left behind us.

As for the officers, most of us being young fellows, and single, we had little to damp our joy at going on foreign service. For my own part, I confess I felt some tender regrets in parting with a fair damsel in the neighbourhood, with whom I was not a little smitten; but I was not of an age to take these matters long to heart, being scarcely sixteen at the time. Poor A—— R—— has since been consigned, by a calculating mother, to an old officer, who had nearly lost his sight, but accumulated a few thousand pounds in the West Indies.

We soon got under way, with a fair wind, for Holland. Instead of being crammed into a transport, with every circumstance which could render a sea-voyage disagreeable, we felt ourselves lucky in being in most comfortable quarters, with a most excellent gentlemanly fellow for our entertainer in Captain Nixon. To add to our comforts, we had the regimental band with us, who were generally playing through the day, when the weather or sear-sickness would allow them. On arriving off Goeree, we were overtaken by one of the most tremendous gales I have ever experienced, and I have had some experience of the element since.

We had come to anchor, expecting a pilot from the shore, between two sandbanks, one on each side of us, while another extended between us and the land. The gale commenced towards night, blowing right on shore; Our awful situation may well be conceived when the wind increased almost to a hurricane, with no hope of procuring a pilot. The sea, which had begun to rise before the commencement of the gale, was now running mountains high, and we could see the white foam, and hear the tremendous roar of the breakers on the sandbank astern of us. Of the two transports which accompanied us with the troops on board, one had anchored outside of us, and the other had been so fortunate as to get out to sea before the gale had reached its greatest violence. We had two anchors a-head, but the sea was so high, that we had but little expectation of holding-on during the night. About midnight, the transport which had come to anchor to windward, drifted past us, having carried away her cables.

The sea every now and then broke over us from stem to stern, and we continued through a great part of the night to fire signals of distress. It is curious to observe on these occasions the different effects of danger on the minds of men: the nervous, alarmed too soon, and preparing themselves for the worst that may happen; the stupid and insensible, without forethought of danger, until they are in the very jaws of destruction, when they are taken quite unprepared, and resign themselves up to despair; and the thoughtless, whose levity inclines them to catch the external expression of the confidence or fear in the countenances of those around them.

About one o'clock in the morning, the captain got into bed, and we followed his example, but had hardly lain down, when the alarm was given that one of the cables was gone. We immediately ran on deck, but it was soon discovered that the wind had shifted a few points, and that the cable had only slackened a little. As the day dawned, the wind gradually abated, and at length fell off to a dead calm. A light haze hid the low land from our view, and hung over the sea, which still rolled in huge billows, as if to conceal the horrors of our situation during the preceding night. In an hour or two, the fog cleared away sufficiently to enable us to see a few miles in all directions.

Every eye was strained in search of the two transports, with our regiment on board, but seeing nothing, we all gave them up for lost; for we could hardly conceive the possibility of the transport, which drifted past us in the night, escaping shipwreck on this low and dangerous coast, or of the other being able to get out to sea. By the help of our sweeps and a light breeze, we were getting more in with the land, when at last we observed a pilot-boat coming out to us. Our little Dutch pilot, when he got alongside of us, soon relieved our minds from anxiety as to the fate of one of the transports, which had fortunately escaped the sandbanks, and was safe in Helvoet Sluys.

A Dutchman being an animal quite new to many of us, we were not a little diverted with his dress and demeanour. Diederick was a little, thick-set, round-built fellow, about five feet three inches in height, bearing a considerable resemblance in shape to his boat: he was so cased up in clothes, that no particular form was to be traced about him, excepting an extraordinary roundness and projection "*a posteriori*" which he owed as much, I believe, to nature as to his habiliments. He wore a tight, coarse, blue jerkin, or pea-jacket, on his body, and reaching halfway down his legs, gathered up in folds tight round his waist, and bunching out amply below. His jacket had no collar, but he had a handkerchief tied round his neck like a rope, which, with his protruding glassy eyes, gave him the appearance of strangulation.

On his legs he wore so many pairs of breeches and trowsers, that I verily believe we might have pulled off three or four pairs without being a whit the wiser as to his natural conformation. On his feet he wore a pair of shoes with huge buckles, and his head was crowned with a high-topped red nightcap.

Thus equipped, with the addition of a short pipe stuck in his mouth, *"ecce"* Diederick, our worthy pilot, who stumping manfully up to the captain, with his hand thrust out like a bowsprit, and a familiar nod of his head, wished him *"goeden dag,"* and welcomed him cordially to Holland. I observed that our captain seemed a little "taken aback" with the pilot's republican manners; however, he did not refuse honest Diederick a shake of his hand, for the latter had evidently no conception of a difference in rank requiring any difference in the mode of salutation. After paying his respects to the captain, he proceeded to shake us all by the hand in turn, with many expressions of goodwill to the English, whom he was pleased to say had *always* been the Dutchmen's best friends. Having completed the ceremonial of our reception, he returned to the binnacle, and, hearing the leadsman sing out "by the mark three," clapping his fat fists to his sides, and looking up to see if the sails were "clean full," exclaimed with great energy, *"Bout Skipp!"*

The captain was anxious to procure some information regarding the channels between the sandbanks, and depth of the water, but all the satisfaction our friend Diederick would vouchsafe him was, *"Ja, Mynheer, wanneer wij niet beter kan maaken dan moeten wij naar de anker komen."* ("When we can't do better we must come to anchor," a common Dutch saying.) We soon reached Helvoet Sluys and came to anchor for the night.

On landing next day, we found the half of the regiment which had so fortunately escaped shipwreck, with the transport which had drifted past us in the night of the gale. Here we took leave of our kind friends the captain and officers of the *Nightingale*, and next day marched to Buitensluys, a little town nearly opposite to Willemstadt. Here we were detained for several days, it not being possible to cross the intervening branch of the sea, in consequence of the quantities of ice which were floating down from the rivers.

We soon got ourselves billeted, out in the town and neighbouring country, and established a temporary mess at the principal inn of the place, where we began to practise the Dutch accomplishments of drinking gin and smoking, for which we had a convenient excuse in the humidity and coldness of the climate. Our hard drinkers, of course, did not fail to inculcate the doctrine, that wine and spirits were the "sovereignest remedy" in the world for the ague, of which disease they seemed to live in constant dread, particularly after dinner. During our sojourn at Buitensluys, our great amusement through the day was skating on the ice with the country girls, who were nothing shy, and played all manners of tricks with us, by upsetting us, &c. &c. thus affording rather a dangerous precedent, which was sometimes returned on themselves with interest.

We are accustomed to hear of the Dutch phlegm, which certainly forms a distinguishing feature in their "physical character;" they are dull and slow in being excited to the strong emotions, but it is a great mistake to suppose that this constitutional sluggishness implies any deficiency in the milder moral virtues. The Dutch, I generally found to possess, in a high degree, the kindly, charitable feelings of human nature, which show themselves to the greater advantage, from the native simplicity of their manners. I had got a comfortable billet at a miller's house, a little out of the village.

The good folks finding that I was a Scotchman, for which people they have a particular liking from some similarity in their manners, began to treat me with great cordiality, and threw off that reserve, which is so natural with people who have soldiers forced into their houses whether they will or not. The miller and his cheerful "*frow*" never tired of showing me every kindness in their power while I remained with them, and to such a degree did they carry this, that it quite distressed me. On leaving Buitensluys, neither my landlord nor his wife would accept of any remuneration, though I urgently pressed it on them. When the avarice of the Dutch character is taken into account, they certainly deserve no small praise for this disinterested kind-heartedness.

The ice having broken up a little, we were enabled to get ferried over to Willemstadt, and proceed on our march to Tholen, where we arrived in two or three days. The cold in Holland this winter was excessive, and Tholen being within four miles of Bergen-op-Zoom, a great part of the inhabitants, as well as garrison, were every day employed in breaking the ice in the ditches of the fortifications. The frost, however, was so intense, that before the circuit was completed, which was towards evening, we were often skating on the places, which had been broken in the morning; we could not, with all our exertions, break more than nine feet in width, which was but an ineffectual protection against the enemy, had they felt any inclination to attack us in this half-dilapidated fortress, with our small garrison.

After we had been here some days, the remainder of our regiment, who had been saved by the transport getting out to sea, joined us. They had sprung a leak, and were near perishing, when it was fortunately stopped, and the gale abated. The first thing we all thought of on coming to Tholen was procuring snug billets, as we might remain some time in garrison. With this view, I employed a German corporal, who acted as our interpreter. He volunteered from the Veteran Battalion at Fort George to accompany us. After looking about for some time, he found out a quarter which he guessed would suit my taste. The house was inhabited by a respectable *burgher*, who had been at sea, and still retained the title of Skipper. His son, as I afterwards learned, had died a few months before, leaving a very pretty young widow, who still resided with her father-in-law. I had not seen her long before I became interested in her.

Johanna M—— was innocence and simplicity itself; tender, soft, and affectionate; her eyes did not possess that brightness which bespeaks lively passions, and too often inconstancy; but they were soft, dark, and liquid, beaming with affection and goodness of heart. On coming home one day, I found her with her head resting on her hands and in tears; her father and mother-in-law, with their glistening eyes resting on her, with an expression of sympathy and sorrow, apparently more for her loss than their own; as if they would have said, "Poor girl! we have lost a son, but you have lost a husband."

Johanna, however, was young, and her spirits naturally buoyant: of course, it cannot be supposed that this intensity of feeling could exist but at intervals. As usual, I soon made myself quite at home with the Skipper and his family, and became, moreover, a considerable favourite, from the interest I took in Johanna, and a talent at making punch, which was always put in requisition when they had a visit from the "*Predikaant*," or priest of the parish; on these occasions I was always one of the party at supper, which is their principal meal. It usually consisted of a large tureen, with bits of meat floating in fat or butter, for which we had to dive with our forks; we had also forcemeat-balls and *sour-crout*.

The priest who was the very picture of good-nature and good-living, wore a three-cornered cocked-hat, which, according to the fashion of the middle classes, never quitted his head, excepting when he said grace. When supper was over and the punch made, which always drew forth the most unqualified praises of the "*Predikaant*" he would lug out a heap of papers from his breeches-pocket, inscribed with favourite Dutch ditties, which, so far as I could understand the language, contained political allusions to the state of matters in Europe at the time. The burden of one of the songs I still remember, from the constant recurrence of the words, "*Well mag het Ue bekoomen*" at the end of each *stanza*. The jolly priest being no singer, always read these overflowings of the Dutch muse with the most energetic gestures and accent.

At the end of each verse, which seemed by its rhyme to have something of the titillating effect of a feather on the sober features of the "Skipper," the reader would break out into a Stentorian laugh, enough to have shaken down the walls of Jericho, or the Stadt-huis itself. The good "*vrow*," whose attention was almost entirely occupied with her household concerns, and who had still more prose in her composition than her mate, would now and then, like a good wife, exhibit some feeble tokens of pleasure, when she observed his features to relax in a more than ordinary degree.

Soon after I had taken up my abode in the house, I observed that Johanna had got a Dutch and English grammar, which she had begun to study with great assiduity, and as I was anxious to acquire Dutch, this naturally enough brought us often together. She would frequently come into my room to ask the pronunciation of some word, for she was particularly scrupulous on this head. On these occasions, I would make her sit down beside me, and endeavour to make her perfect in each word in succession; but she found so much difficulty in bringing her pretty lips into the proper form, that I was under the necessity of enforcing my instructions, by punishing her with a kiss for every failure. But so far was this from quickening her apprehension, that the difficulties seemed to increase at every step.

Poor Johanna, notwithstanding this little innocent occupation, could not, however, be entirely weaned from her affection for the memory of her departed husband, for her grief would often break out in torrents of tears; when this was the case, we had no lesson for that day. Garrison duty is always dull and irksome, and soldiers are always glad of anything to break the monotony of a life where there is no activity or excitement. One day, while we lay at Tholen, a letter was brought from headquarters, which was to be forwarded from town to town to Admiral Young, who was lying in the Scheldt at the time.

A couple of horses and a guide were procured, and I was sent with the letter, much to my own satisfaction, as I was glad of an opportunity to see more of the country. I was ordered to proceed to a certain town, the name of which I forget, where another officer should relieve me. It was late when I got to the town, and not being aware that it was occupied by a Russian regiment, I was not a little surprised in being challenged by a sentry in a foreign language. I could not make out from the soldier what they were, until the officer of the guard came up, who understood a little English. He informed me that they were on their march to Tholen, where they were to do garrison duty.

On desiring to be conducted to his commanding officer, he brought me to the principal house in the town, at the door of which two sentries were posted. The scene in the interior was singular enough. The first object that met my eyes on entering the colonel's apartment, was a knot of soldiers in their green jackets and trowsers, lying in a heap, one above another, in the corner of the room, (with their bonnets pulled over their eyes,) like a litter of puppies, and snoring like bull-frogs. These were the colonel's body-guard.

The room with its furniture exhibited a scene of the most outrageous debauchery. Chairs overturned, broken decanters and bottles, fragments of tumblers and wine-glasses lay scattered over the floor and table. Two or three candles were still burning on the table, and others had been broken in the conflict of bottles and other missiles. Taking a rapid glance at the state of matters in passing, we approached the colonel's bed, which stood in one corner of the room. My conductor drew the curtains, when I saw two people lying in their flannel-shirts; the elder was a huge, broad-faced man, with a ferocious expression of countenance, who I was informed was the colonel; the other was a young man about seventeen years of age, exceedingly handsome, and with so delicate a complexion, that I actually thought at the time he must be the colonel's wife.

With this impression I drew back for a moment, when he spoke to me in good English, and told me he was the adjutant, and begged I would state what I had to communicate to the colonel, which he would interpret to him, as the latter did not understand English. The colonel said he should forward the letter by one of his officers, and as I could then return to Tholen, we should proceed to that place next morning. We proceeded accordingly next morning on our march to

BATTALION INFANTRY,
6TH or 1ST WARWICKSHIRE REGIMENT,
23RD or ROYAL WELSH FUSILEERS.

Tholen. The colonel had sent on his light company as an advanced-guard, some time before us, with orders to halt at a village on the road, until the regiment came up. Whether they had mistaken his orders I know not, but on coming to the village, no light company was to be found; and on inquiry, we learned that they had marched on.

The rage of the colonel knew no bounds and produced a most ridiculous and childish scene betwixt himself and the officers. With the tears running down his cheeks, and stamping with rage, he went among them; first accusing one, and then the other, as if they were to blame for the mistake of the advanced-guard. Each of them, however, answered him in a petulant snappish manner, like enraged pug-dogs, at the same time clapping their hands to their swords, and some of them drawing them half out of the scabbards, when he would turn away from them, weeping bitterly like a great blubbering boy all the while.

The officers, however, began to pity the poor colonel, and at last succeeded in appeasing his wrath and drying his tears. He proceeded forthwith to order an enormous breakfast to be prepared for us immediately. It was of no use for the innkeeper to say that he had not any of the articles they desired, he was compelled by threats and curses to procure them, come whence they would. As our landlord knew well whom he had to deal with, our table soon groaned under a load of dishes, enough apparently to have dined four times our number. In a trice we had everything that could be procured for love or money, and it was wonderful to observe with what alacrity the landlord waited on us and obeyed the orders he received. He appeared, in fact, to have thrown off his native sluggishness, and two or three pairs of breeches for the occasion.

Before proceeding on the march, I wished to pay my share of the entertainment, but my proposal was treated with perfect ridicule. At first, I imagined that the Russians considered me as their guest, but I could not discover that the innkeeper received any remuneration for the entertainment prepared for us. The Russians had many odd customs during their meals, such as drinking out of each other's glasses, and eating from each other's plates; a compliment, which in England, we could willingly dispense with. They seemed to have a great liking to the English, and every day our men and theirs were seen walking arm-in-arm about the streets together. The gin, which was rather too cheap in this country, seemed to be a great bond of union between them; and strange to say, I do not recollect a single instance of their quarrelling.

Notwithstanding the snapping between the commanding officer and the other officers, they seemed on the whole to be in excellent discipline in other respects. The manner in which they went through their exercise was admirable, particularly when we consider that they were only sailors acting on shore. There was one custom, however, which never failed to excite our disgust and indignation; hardly a day passed but we saw some of their officers boxing the ears of their men in the ranks, who seemed to bear this treatment with the greatest patience, and without turning their eyes to the right or left during the operation; but such is the effect of early habits and custom, that the very men who bore this degrading treatment, seemed to feel the same disgust for our military punishment of flogging; which, however degrading in its effects on the character of the sufferer, could not at least be inflicted at the caprice of the individual. We may here observe the different effects produced on the character of men by a free and a despotic system of government: it was evidently not the nature, but the degree, of punishment in our service which shocked the Russian prejudices.

We had all become thoroughly sick of the monotony and sameness of our duties and occupations at Tholen, when we received orders to march the next day, (8th March, 1814). As the attack on Bergen-op-Zoom, which took place on that evening, was of course kept a profound secret, the common opinion was, that we were destined for Antwerp, where the other division of the army had already had some fighting. Though elated, in common with my brother officers, with the prospect of coming to closer quarters with the enemy, it was not without tears on both sides that I parted with poor Johanna, who had somehow taken a hold of my affections that I was hardly aware of till this moment.

The time left us to prepare for our march I devoted to her, and she did not even seek the pretext of her English grammar to remain in my room for the few hours we could yet enjoy together. We had marched some miles before I could think of anything but her, for the recollection of her tears still thrilled to my very heart and occasioned a stifling sensation that almost deprived me of utterance. But we were soon thrown into a situation where the excitement was too powerful and engrossing to leave room for other thoughts than of what we were immediately engaged in.

It was nearly dark when we arrived at the village of Halteren, which is only three or four miles from Bergen-op-Zoom, where we took up our quarters for the night. On the distribution of the billets to the officers for the night, I received one upon a farmhouse about a mile in the country. I had not been long at my new lodging, when I was joined by four or five officers of the 4th Battalion Royal Scots, who had just arrived by long marches from Stralsund, and were billeted about the country. They had heard that an attempt to surprise Bergen-op-Zoom would be made that same night. It is not easy to describe the sensations occasioned in my mind by this intelligence; it certainly partook but little of fear, but the novelty (to me at least) of the situation in which we were about to be placed, excited a feeling of anxiety as to the result of an attempt, in which, from the known strength of the place, we dared hardly expect to be successful.

There is also a degree of melancholy which takes hold of the mind at these moments of serious reflection which precede the conflict. My comrades evidently shared this feeling with me. One of them remarked, as we were preparing to march, "My boys, we'el see something like service tonight," and added, "we'el not all meet again in this world."

Poor MacNicol, who made the remark, fell that night, which was the first and the last of my acquaintance with him. I believe every one of us were wounded. Learning from my new acquaintances that the grenadier company of their regiment, (Royal Scots), which was commanded by an old friend of mine, (Lieutenant Allan Robertson,) and whom I had not seen for some years, was only about a mile farther off, I thought I should have time to see him and join my regiment before they marched, should they be sent to the attack. However, the party of the Royals whom I accompanied lost their way, from their ignorance of the road, and we in consequence made a long circuit, during which I heard from an *aide-de-camp* who passed us, that the 21st were on their march to attack the place on another quarter from us.

In these circumstances I was exceedingly puzzled what course to take; if I went in search of my regiment, I had every chance of missing them in the night, being quite ignorant of the roads. Knowing that the Royals would be likely to head one of the columns from the number of the regiment, I took what I thought the surest plan, by attaching myself to the grenadier company under my gallant friend. There is something awfully impressive in the mustering of soldiers before going into action; many of those names, which the sergeants were now calling in an under tone of voice, would never be repeated, but in the tales of their comrades who saw them fall.

BRITISH GUARDS

After mustering the men, we proceeded to the general "rendezvous" of the regiments forming the column; the Royals led the column followed by the other regiments according to their number. As everything depended on our taking the enemy by surprise, the strictest orders were given to observe a profound silence on the march.

While we are proceeding to the attack, it will not be amiss to give the reader a slight sketch of the situation of Bergen-op-Zoom, and the plan of the operations of the different columns, to render my relation of the proceedings of the column I served with the more intelligible.

Bergen-op-Zoom is situated on the right bank of the Scheldt, and takes its name from the little river Zoom, which, after supplying the defences with water, discharges itself into the Scheldt. The old channel of the Zoom, into which the tide flows towards the centre of the town, forms the harbour, which is nearly dry at low-water. The mouth of the harbour was the point fixed upon for the attack of the right column, under Major-General Skerret, and Brig.-Gen. Gore. This column consisted of 1100 men of the 1st regiment, or Royal Scots, the 37th, 44th, and 91st, (as far as I can recollect). Lieut.-Col. Henry, with 650 men of the 21st, or Royal Scot's Fusiliers, was sent on a false attack near the Steenbergen-gate, to the left of the harbour, (I suppose the reader to be standing at the entrance of the harbour facing the town). Another column, consisting of 1200 men of the 33d, 55th, and 69th regiments, under Lieut.-Col. Morrice, were to attack the place near the Bredagate, and endeavour to enter by escalade.

A third column, under Col. Lord Proby, consisting of 1000 men of the 1st and Coldstream Guards, was to make nearly a complete circuit of the place, and enter the enemy's works by crossing the ice, some distance to the right of the entrance of the harbour and the Waterport-gate. This slight account of the plan of attack I have borrowed in some degree from Col. Jones' *Narrative*, (included in this edition), who must have procured his information on these points from the best sources. However, as I only pretend to speak with certainty of what fell under my own immediate observation, I shall return to the right column, with which I served on this occasion.

When we had proceeded some way, we fell in with a picket, commanded by Capt. Darrah, of the 21st. Fusiliers, who was mustering his men to proceed to the attack. Thinking that our regiment (the 21st), must pass his post on their way to the false attack, he told me to remain with him until they came up. I, in consequence, waited some time, but hearing nothing of the regiment, and losing patience, I gave him the slip in the dark, and ran on until I regained my place with the grenadier company of the Royals. On approaching the place of attack, we crossed the Tholen-dike, and immediately entered the bed of the Zoom, through which we had to push our way before we entered the wet ditch. It is not easy to convey an idea of the toil we experienced in getting through the deep mud of the river; we immediately sank nearly to our middles, and when, with great difficulty, we succeeded in freeing one leg from the mire, we sank nearly to the shoulder on the other side before we could get one pace forward.

As might be expected, we got into some confusion in labouring through this horrible slough, which was like bird-lime about our legs; regiments got intermixed in the darkness, while some stuck fast, and some unlucky wretches got trodden down and smothered in the mud. Notwithstanding this obstruction, a considerable portion of the column had got through, when those behind us, discouraged by this unexpected difficulty, raised a shout to encourage themselves. Gen. Skerret, who was at the head of the column, was furious with rage, but the mischief was already done. The sluices were opened, and a torrent of water poured down on us through the channel of the river, by which the progress of those behind was effectually stopped for some time.

Immediately after the sluices were opened, a brilliant firework was displayed on the ramparts, which showed every object as clearly as daylight. Several cannon and some musketry opened on us, but did us little harm, as they seemed to be discharged at random. At the moment the water came down, I had just cleared the deepest part of the channel, and making a great effort, I gained a flat piece of ice which was sticking edgeways in the mud; to this I clung till the strength of the torrent had passed, after which I soon gained the firm land, and pushed on with the others to the ditch. The point at which we entered was a bastion to the right of the harbour, from one of the angles of which a row of high palisades was carried through the ditch. To enable us to pass the water, some scaling-ladders had been sunk to support us in proceeding along the palisade, over which we had first to climb with each other's assistance, our soldiers performing the office of ladders to those who preceded them.

So great were the obstacles we met with, that had not the attention of the enemy fortunately (or rather most judiciously), been distracted by the false attack under Col. Henry, it appeared quite impossible for us to have affected an entrance at this point. While we were proceeding forward in this manner, Col. Muller of the Royals, (now of the Ceylon regiment), was clambering along the tops of the palisade, calling to those who had got the start of him, to endeavour to open the Waterport-gate, and let down the drawbridge to our right; but no one in the hurry of the moment seemed to hear him. On getting near enough, I told him I should effect it if it was possible.

We met with but trifling resistance on gaining the rampart; the enemy being panic struck, fled to the streets and houses in the town, from which they kept up a pretty sharp fire on us for some time. I got about twenty soldiers of different regiments to follow me to the Waterport-gate, which we found closed. It was constructed of thin paling, with an iron bar across it about three inches in breadth. Being without tools of any kind, we made several ineffectual attempts to open it. At last, retiring a few paces, we made a rush at it in a body, when the iron bar snapped in the middle like a bit of glass. Some of my people got killed and wounded during this part of the work, but when we got to the drawbridge, we were a little more sheltered from the firing.

The bridge was up and secured by a lock in the right-hand post of the two which supported it. I was simple enough to attempt to pick the lock with a soldier's bayonet, but after breaking two or three, we at last had an axe brought us from the bastion where the troops were entering. With the assistance of this instrument we soon succeeded in cutting the lock out of the post, and taking hold of the chain, I had the satisfaction to pull down the drawbridge with my own hands.

While I was engaged in this business, Col. Muller was forming the Royals on the rampart where we entered; but a party of about 150 men of different regiments, under General Skerret, who must have entered to the left of the harbour, were clearing the ramparts towards the Steinbergen-gate, where the false attack had been made under Col. Henry; and a party, also, under Col. Carleton, of the 44th regiment, was proceeding in the opposite direction along the ramparts to the right, without meeting with much resistance. Hearing the firing on the opposite side of the town from Gen. Skerret's party, and supposing that they had marched through the town, I ran on through the streets to overtake them, accompanied by only one or two soldiers, for the rest had left me and returned to the bastion after we had opened the gate.

In proceeding along the canal or harbour, which divided this part of the town, I came to a loop-holed wall, which was continued from the houses down to the water's edge. I observed a party of soldiers within a gate in this wall, and was going up to them, taking them for our own people, when I was challenged in French, and had two or three shots fired at me. Seeing no other way of crossing the harbour but by a little bridge, which was nearly in a line with the wall, I returned to the Waterport-gate, which I found Col. Muller had taken possession of with two or three companies of his regiment. I went up to him and told him that I had opened the gate according to his desire, and of the interruption I had met with in the town. Not knowing me, he asked my name, which he said he would remember, and sent one of the companies up with me to the wall, already mentioned, and ordered the officer who commanded the company, after he should have driven the enemy away, to keep possession of it until farther orders. On coming to the gate, we met with a sharp resistance, but after firing a few rounds, and preparing to charge they gave way, leaving us in possession of the gate and bridge.

Leaving the company here, and crossing the little bridge, I again set forward alone to overtake Gen. Skerret's party, guided by the firing on the ramparts. Avoiding any little parties of the enemy, I had reached the inside of the ramparts where the firing was, without its occurring to me that I might get into the wrong box and be taken prisoner. Fortunately, I observed a woman looking over a shop door, on one side of the street; the poor creature, who must have been under the influence of some strong passion to remain in her present exposed situation, was pale and trembling. She was a Frenchwoman, young, and not bad looking. I asked her where the British soldiers were, which she told me without hesitation, pointing at the same time in the direction. I shook hands with her, and bade her goodnight, not entertaining the smallest suspicion of her deceiving me; following her directions, I clambered up the inside of the rampart, and rejoined Gen. Skerret's party.

The moon had now risen, and though the sky was cloudy, we could see pretty well what was doing. I found my friend Robertson here, with the grenadier company of the Royals; I learned from him that the party, which was now commanded by Capt. Guthrie of the 33rd regiment, had been compelled by numbers to retire from the bastion which the enemy now occupied, and should endeavour to maintain the one which they now possessed, until they could procure a reinforcement. He also told me of Gen. Skerret's being dangerously wounded and taken prisoner, an irreparable loss to our party, as Capt. Guthrie was ignorant of the general's intentions. In the meantime, the enemy continued a sharp firing on us, which we returned as fast as our men could load their firelocks.

Several of the enemy who had fallen, as well as of our own men, were lying on the ramparts; one of our officers, who had been wounded in the arm, was walking about, saying occasionally, in rather a discontented manner, "This is what is called honour;" though I could readily sympathise with him in the pain he suffered, I could not exactly understand how, if there is any honour in getting wounded, any bodily suffering can detract from it.

We found a large pile of logs of wood on the rampart; these we immediately disposed across the gorge of the bastion, so as to form a kind of parapet, over which our people could fire, leaving, however, about half the distance open towards the parapet of the rampart. On the opposite side of the bastion were two twenty-four-pounders of the enemy's, which being raised on high platforms, we turned upon them, firing along the ramparts over the heads of our own party. However valuable this resource might be to us, we were still far from being on equal terms with the French, who besides greatly exceeding us in numbers, had also brought up two or three fieldpieces, which annoyed us much during the night.

There was also a windmill on the bastion they occupied, from the top of which their musketry did great execution among us. In the course of the night, they made several ineffectual attempts to drive us from our position: on these occasions, which we always were aware of from the shouts they raised to encourage each other, as soon as they made their appearance on the rampart, we gave them a good dose of grape from our twenty-four-pounders and had a party ready to charge them back. I observed our soldiers were always disposed to meet the enemy half-way, and the latter were soon so well aware of our humour, that they invariably turned tail before we could get within forty or fifty paces of them.

The firing was kept up almost continually on both sides until about two o'clock in the morning, when it would sometimes cease for more than half-an-hour together. During one of these intervals of stillness, exhausted with our exertions, and the cold we felt in our drenched clothes, some of the officers and I lay down along the parapet together, in hopes of borrowing a little heat from each other. I fell insensibly into a troubled dozing state, in which my imagination still revelled in the scenes of night. While I yet lay the firing had recommenced, which, with the shouts of the enemy, and the words of those about me, seemed to form but the ground work of my fitful dream, which

FRENCH INFANTRY

continued to link imaginary circumstances to reality.

How long I might have lain in this stupor, between sleeping and waking, I know not, when suddenly I felt the ground shake under me, and heard at the same time a crash as if the whole town had been overwhelmed by an earthquake; a bright glare of light burst on my eyes at the same instant and almost blinded me. A shot from the enemy had blown up our small magazine on the ramparts, on which we depended for the supply of the two twenty-four-pounders which had been of such material use to us during the night. This broke our slumbers most effectually; and we had now nothing for it but to maintain our ground in the best way we were able until we could receive a reinforcement from some of the other parties.

Immediately after this disaster, raising a tremendous shout or rather yell, the enemy again attempted to come to close quarters with us, in hopes of our being utterly disheartened; but our charging party, which we had always in readiness, made them wheel round as usual. In the course of the night, we had sent several small parties of men to represent the state of our detachment, and endeavour to procure assistance, but none of them returned, having, we supposed, been intercepted by the enemy. Discouraged as we were by this circumstance, we still continued to hold our ground until break of day.

By this time the firing had entirely ceased in the other part of the town, naturally leading us, in the absence of all communication, to conclude that the other parties had been driven from the place. However, this may have been, the first dawn of day showed us in but too plain colours the hopelessness of our situation. The enemy now brought an overwhelming force against us; but still we expected, from the narrowness of the rampart, that they would not be able to derive the full advantage of their superiority; but in this we were deceived. The bastion we occupied was extensive, but only that portion of it near the gorge was furnished with a parapet.

At this spot, and behind the logs which we had thrown up, our now diminished force was collected. Keeping up an incessant fire to divert our attention, the French (who now outnumbered us, at least three to one,) detached a part of their force, which skirting the outside of the ramparts, and ascending the face of the bastion we occupied, suddenly opened a most destructive fire on our flank and rear. From this latter party we were totally unprotected, while they were sheltered by the top of the rampart: we were thus left to defend ourselves from both at once as we best could. But still they would not venture to charge us, and it would have been of little use for us to charge them, for the moment we quitted the parapet, we would have been exposed to a cross fire from the other bastion.

The slaughter was now dreadful, and our poor fellows, who had done all that soldiers could in our trying situation, now fell thick and fast. Just at this moment, my friend Robertson, under whose command I had put myself at the beginning of the attack, fell. I had just time to run up to him and found him stunned from a wound in the head; when our gallant commander, seeing the inutility of continuing the unequal contest, gave the order to retreat. We had retired in good order about three hundred yards, when poor Guthrie received a wound in the head, which I have since been informed deprived him of his sight.

The enemy, when they saw us retreating, hung upon our rear, keeping up a sharp fire all the time, but they still seemed to have some respect for us from the trouble we had already given them. We had indulged the hope, that by continuing our course along the ramparts, we should be able to effect our retreat by the Waterport-gate, (this was the only gate which was opened during the night), not being aware that we should be intercepted by the mouth of the harbour. We were already at the very margin before we discovered our mistake and completely hemmed in by the French. We had therefore no alternative left to us but to surrender ourselves prisoners of war, or to attempt to effect our escape across the harbour, by means of the floating pieces of ice with which the water was covered.

Not one of us seemed to entertain the idea of surrender, however, and in the despair, which had now taken possession of every heart, we threw ourselves into the water, or leaped for the broken pieces of ice which were floating about. The scene that ensued was shocking beyond description—the canal or harbour was faced on both sides by high brick walls—in the middle of the channel lay a small Dutch decked vessel, which was secured by a rope to the opposite side of the harbour. Our only hope of preserving our lives or effecting our escape, depended on our being able to gain this little vessel.

Already, many had, by leaping first on one piece of ice and then on another, succeeded in getting on board the vessel, which they drew to the opposite side of the canal by the rope, and thus freed one obstruction: but immediately afterwards, being intercepted by the Waterport redoubt, they were compelled to surrender. The soldiers in particular, when they found themselves enclosed by the enemy, seemed to lose the power of reflection, and leaped madly into the water, with their arms in their hands, without even waiting until a piece of ice should float within their reach. The air was rent with vain cries for help from the drowning soldiers, mixed with the exulting shouts of the enemy, who seemed determined to make us drain the bitter cup of defeat to the very dregs.

Among the rest I had scrambled down the face of the canal to a beam running horizontally along the brick-work, from which other beams descended perpendicularly into the water, to prevent the sides from being injured by sniping. After sticking my sword into my belt, (for I had thrown the scabbard away the previous night,) I leaped from this beam, which was nine or ten feet above the water, for a piece of ice, but not judging my distance very well, it tilted up with me, and I sunk to the bottom of the water. However, I soon came up again, and after swimming to the other side of the canal and to the vessel, I found nothing to catch hold of. I had therefore nothing for it but to hold on by the piece of ice I had at first leaped on, and swinging my body under it, I managed to keep my face out of the water.

I had just caught hold of the ice in time, for encumbered as I was with a heavy great coat, now thoroughly soaked, I was in a fair way to share the fate of many a poor fellow now lying at the bottom of the water. I did not, however, retain my slippery hold undisturbed. I was several times dragged under water by the convulsive grasp of the drowning soldiers, but by desperate efforts I managed to free myself and regain my hold. Even at this moment, I cannot think without horror of the means which the instinct of self-preservation suggested to save my own life, while some poor fellow clung to my clothes: I think I still see his agonized look, and hear his imploring cry, as he sank for ever.

After a little time, I remained undisturbed tenant of the piece of ice. I was not, however, the only survivor of those who had got into the water; several of them were still hanging on to other pieces of ice, but they one by one let go their hold, and sank as their strength failed. At length only three or four besides myself remained. All this time some of the enemy continued firing at us, and I saw one or two shot in the water near me. So intent was everyone on effecting his escape, that though they sometimes cast a look of commiseration at their drowning comrades, no one thought for a moment of giving us any assistance. The very hope of it had at length so completely faded in our minds, that we had ceased to ask the aid of those that passed us on the fragments of ice. But Providence had reserved one individual who possessed a heart to feel for the distress of his fellow-creatures more than for his own personal safety.

The very last person that reached the vessel in the manner I have already described, was Lieut. M'Dougal, of the 91st Regiment. I had attracted his attention in passing me, and he had promised his assistance when he should reach the vessel. He soon threw me a rope, but I was now so weak, and benumbed with the intense cold, that it slipped through my fingers alongside of the vessel; he then gave me another, doubled, which I got under my arms, and he thus succeeded, with the assistance of a wounded man, in getting me on board.

I feel that it is quite out of my power to do justice to the humanity and contempt of danger displayed by our generous deliverer on this occasion. While I was assisting him in saving the two or three soldiers who still clung to pieces of ice, I got a musket-ball through my wrist; for all this time several of the enemy continued deliberately firing at us from the opposite rampart, which was not above sixty yards from the vessel.

Not content with what he had already done for me, my kind-hearted friend insisted on helping me out of the vessel; but I could not consent to his remaining longer exposed to the fire of the enemy, who had already covered the deck with killed and wounded, and M'Dougal fortunately still remained unhurt. Finding that I would not encumber him, he left the vessel, and I went down to the cabin, where I found Lieut. Briggs, of the 91st, sitting on one side, with a severe wound through his shoulder-blade. The floor of the cabin was covered with water, for the vessel had become leaky from the firing. I took my station on the opposite side, and taking off my neckcloth, with the assistance of my teeth, I managed to bind up my wound, so as to stop the bleeding in some measure. My companion suffered so much from his wound that little conversation passed betwixt us.

I fell naturally into gloomy reflections on the events of the night. I need hardly say how bitter and mortifying they were: after all our toils and sanguine anticipations of ultimate success, to be thus robbed of the prize which we already grasped, as we thought, with a firm hand. Absorbed in these melancholy ruminations, accompanied from time to time by a groan from my companion, several hours passed away, during which the water continued rising higher and higher in the cabin, until it reached my middle, and I was obliged to hold my arm above it, for the salt-water made it smart. Fortunately, the vessel grounded from the receding of the tide. Escape in our state being now quite out of the question, my companion and I were glad on the whole to be relieved from our present disagreeable situation by surrendering ourselves prisoners.

The firing had now entirely ceased, and the French seemed satiated with the ample vengeance they had taken on us. As there was no gate near us, we were hoisted with ropes over the ramparts, which were here faced with brick to the top. A French soldier was ordered to show me the way to the hospital in the town. As we proceeded, however, my guide took a fancy to my canteen which still hung by my side, and laying hold of it without ceremony, was proceeding to empty its contents into his own throat. Though suffering with a burning thirst from loss of blood, I did not recollect till this moment that there was about two-thirds of a bottle of gin remaining in it. I immediately snatched it from the fellow's hand and clapping it to my mouth, finished every drop of it at a draught, while he vented his rage in oaths. I found it exceedingly refreshing, but it had no more effect on my nerves than small beer in my present state of exhaustion.

The scene as we passed through the streets, strewed here and there with the bodies of our fallen soldiers, intermixed with those of the enemy, was, indeed, melancholy; even could I have forgotten for a moment how the account stood between the enemy and us, I was continually reminded of our failure, by the bodies of many of our people being already stripped of their upper garments. When we arrived at the hospital, I found one of the officers of my regiment, who had been taken prisoner, standing at the door. My face was so plastered with blood from a prick of a bayonet I had got in the temple from one of our soldiers, that it was some time before he knew me. In passing along the beds in the hospital, the first face I recognised was that of my friend Robertson, whom I had left for dead when our party retreated. Besides the wound he received in the head, he had received one in the wrist, after he fell.

On lying down on the bed prepared for me, I was guilty of a piece of simplicity, which I had ample occasion to repent before I left the place. I took all my clothes off and sent them to be dried by the people of the hospital, but they were never returned to me. I was in consequence forced to keep my bed for the three days I remained prisoner in Bergen-op-Zoom.

The hospital was crowded with the wounded on both sides. On my right hand lay Ensign Martial of the 55th regiment, with a grape-

FRENCH INFANTRY AND EAGLE

shot wound in his shoulder, of which, and ague together, he afterwards died at Klundert. On my left, in an adjoining room, lay poor General Skerret, with a desperate wound through the body, of which he died next night. It was said that he might have recovered, had it not been for the bruises he had received from the muskets of the enemy after he fell. This story I can hardly credit. However, that may be, there is no doubt we lost in him a most gallant, zealous, and active officer, and at a most unfortunate time for the success of the enterprise. On the opposite side of the hospital lay Capt. Campbell, of the 55th regiment. He had a dreadful wound from a grape which entered at his shoulder and went out near the backbone. He was gifted with the most extraordinary flow of spirits of any man I have ever met with. He never ceased talking from sun-rise till night and afforded all of us who were in a condition to relish anything, an infinite deal of amusement. I had told Campbell of the trick they had played me with my clothes, and it immediately became with him a constant theme for rating every Frenchman that passed him.

In the course of the next day a French sergeant came swaggering into the hospital, with an officer's sash tied round him, and stretched out to its utmost breadth. He boasted that he had killed the officer by whom it had been worn. Twice a day two of the attendants of the hospital went about with buckets in their hands, one containing small pieces of boiled meat, which was discovered to be horseflesh by the medical people, while another contained a miserable kind of stuff, which they called soup, and a third contained bits of bread. One of the pieces of meat was tossed on each bed with a fork in passing; but the patient had always to make his choice between flesh and bread, and soup and bread, it being thought too much to allow them soup and meat at the same time.

I was never so much puzzled in my life as by this alternative. Constantly tormented with thirst, I usually asked for soup, but my hunger, with which I was no less tormented, made me as often repent my choice. While we lay here we were attended by our own surgeons, and had every attention paid to us in this respect that we could desire.

In the meantime, arrangements were entered into with Gen. Bizanet, the French commander, for an exchange of prisoners, and in consequence the last of the wounded prisoners were removed in waggons to Rozendaal, on the third day after we had been taken. On this occasion I was obliged to borrow a pair of trowsers from one of the soldiers, and a coat from my neighbour Martial, of the 55th, who being a tall man and I rather little, it reached halfway down my legs. Altogether I cut rather an odd figure as I started from the hospital. My regimental cap and shoes had, however, escaped the fate of my other habiliments, so, considering circumstances, matters might have been worse.

But, one trial to my temper still remained which I did not expect: the old rascal, to whom I delivered my clothes when I sent them to be dried, had the unparalleled impudence to make a demand on me for the hospital shirt, with which, in place of my own wet one, I had been supplied on entering the hospital. I was so provoked at this unconscionable request, that I believe I should have answered him with a box on the ear, but my only available hand was too well employed at the time in supporting my trowsers.

There was still another reason for my objecting to his demand: before I was taken prisoner, while lying in the vessel, I had managed to conceal some money which happened to be in my pockets on going to the attack; this I had carefully transferred, with due secrecy, to the inferior margin of the hospital shirt in which it was tied with a garter, when we were preparing to leave the place. This treasure, though not large, was of some importance to me, and I determined that nothing short of brute force should deprive me of it. My gentleman, however, pertinaciously urged his claim to the aforesaid garment, and a violent altercation ensued between us, in which I had an opportunity of showing a proficiency in Dutch swearing, that I was not aware of myself till this moment. My friend Campbell came up at last to my assistance, and discharged such a volley of oaths at the old vampire, that he was fairly beaten out of the field, and I carried away the shirt in triumph,

We were marched out of the town by the Breda-gate to Rozendaal, a distance of about fifteen miles, where we arrived the same night. The French soldiers who had fallen in the conflict had all been removed by this time, but, as we proceeded, escorted by the victors, many a ghastly corpse of our countrymen met our half-averted eyes. They had all been more or less stripped of their clothing, and some had only their shirts left for a covering and were turned on their faces. My heart rose at this humiliating spectacle, nor could I breathe freely until we reached the open fields beyond the fortifications. All who were unable to march were crowded into the waggons which had been prepared for them, while those who were less disabled straggled along the road the best way they could. As may be supposed, there were no needless competitors for the waggon conveyance, for the roads were rough, and every jolt of the vehicles produced groans of agony from the wretched passengers.

On arriving at Wouw, which I took in my way, I explained my absence from the regiment to the satisfaction of the commanding officer. I soon heard of the fate of poor Bulteel, (2nd Lieutenant 21st Regiment,) who fell during this ill-starred enterprise, by a cannon-ball, which carried off the top of his head. Never was a comrade more sincerely lamented by his messmates than this most amiable young man. His brother, an officer in the Guards, whom he had met only a few days before, fell the same night. The captain of my company, and kind friend, M'Kenzie, had his leg shattered by a shot on the same occasion, and I was informed that he bore the amputation without suffering a groan to escape from him. Four others were more slightly wounded. The dead had all been collected in the church, and a long trench being dug by the soldiers, they were all next day deposited in the earth without parade, and in silence. In a few days I proceeded to Rozendaal, where, for the present, the prisoners were to remain.

At this place I had more cause than ever to feel grateful for the kindness of my Dutch landladies and landlords; the surgeon who attended me finding it necessary to put me on low diet, and to keep my bed, the sympathy of the good people of the house knew no bounds; not an hour passed but they came to inquire how I was. So disinterested was their unwearied attention, that on leaving them I could not induce them to accept the smallest remuneration. After some time, we went to Klundert, where we were to remain until our exchange should be effected.

Before concluding my narrative of the unfortunate attack on Bergen-op-Zoom, the reader may expect some observations relative to the plan of attack, and the causes of its ultimate failure; but it should be remembered, before venturing to give my opinions on the subject, that nothing is more difficult for an individual attached to any one of the different columns which composed the attacking force, than to assign causes for such an unexpected result, particularly when the communication between them has been interrupted. In a battle in the open field, where every occurrence either takes place under the immediate observation of the General, or is speedily communicated to him, faults can be soon remedied, or at least it may be afterwards determined with some degree of accuracy where they existed.

But in a night attack on a fortified place, the case is very different. As the general of the army cannot be personally present in the attack, any blame which may attach to the undertaking, can only affect him in so far as the original plan is concerned; and if this plan succeeds so far that the place is actually surprised, and the attacking force has effected a lodgment within it, and even been in possession of the greater part of the place, with a force equal to that of the enemy, no candid observer can attribute the failure to any defect in the arrangements of the general. Nothing certainly can be easier than, after the event, to point out certain omissions which, had the general been gifted with the spirit of prophecy, might possibly, in the existing state of matters, have led to a happier result; but nothing, in my humble opinion, can be more unfair, or more uncandid, than to blame the unsuccessful commander, when every possible turn which things might take was not provided against, and while it still remains a doubt how far the remedies proposed by such critics would have succeeded in the execution.

According to the plan of operations, as stated in Sir Thomas Graham's dispatch, it was directed that the right column, under Major-General Skerret, and Brig.-General Gore, which entered at the mouth of the harbour, and the left column under Lord Proby, which Major General Cooke accompanied in person, and which attacked between the Waterport and Antwerp gates, should move along the ramparts and form a junction. This junction, however, did not take place, as General Cooke had been obliged to change the point of attack, which prevented his gaining the ramparts until half-past eleven o'clock, an hour after General Skerret entered with the right column; a large detachment of which, under Colonel the Hon. George Carleton, and General Gore, had, unknown to him, (General Cooke), as it would appear, penetrated along the ramparts far beyond the point where he entered.

The centre column, under Lieut.-Colonel Morrice, which had attacked near the Steenbergen lines, being repulsed with great loss, and a still longer delay occurring before they entered by the scaling-ladders of General Cooke's column, the enemy had ample opportunities to concentrate their force, near the points in most danger. However, notwithstanding all these delays and obstructions, we succeeded (as already stated) in establishing a force equal to that of the enemy along the ramparts. But still, without taking into account the advantage which the attacking force always possesses in the alarm and distraction of the enemy, (which, however, was more than counterbalanced by our entire ignorance of the place,) we could not, in fact, be said to have gained any decided superiority over our adversaries; on the contrary, the chances were evidently against our being able to maintain our position through the night, or until reinforcements could come up.

"But why," I have heard it often urged, "were we not made better acquainted with the place?" In answer to this question, it may be observed, that though there can be no doubt that the leaders of the different columns, at least, had seen plans of the place, yet there is a great difference between a personal knowledge of a place, and that derived from the best plans, even by daylight; but in the night the enemy must possess a most decided advantage over their assailants, in their intimate knowledge of all the communications through the town, as well as in their acquaintance with the bearings of the different works which surround it.

Another circumstance which must have tended most materially to the unfortunate result of the attack was, that the two parties, which had been detached from the right column, were deprived of their commanders in the very beginning of the night, by the fall of Generals Skerret and Gore, and Colonel Carleton. The reader, were I inclined to account for our failure, by these early calamities alone, need not go far to find instances in history where the fate of an army has been decided by the fall of its leader.

There are some statements, however, in the excellent account published by Colonel Jones, (who must have had the best means of information on these points), which irresistibly lead the mind to certain conclusions, which, while they tend most directly to exonerate Sir Thomas Graham, as well as the general entrusted with the command of the enterprise, from the blame which has so unfairly been heaped on them, at the same time seem to imply some degree of misconduct on the part of the battalion detached by General Cooke to support the reserve of 600 men under Lt. Col. Muller at the Waterport gate. This battalion, he (Colonel Jones), states, perceiving the enemy preparing to attack them after having got possession of the Waterport-gate, left the place, by crossing the ice. No reason is given why this battalion did not fall back on General Cooke's force at the Orange bastion.

The surrender of the reserve at the Waterport-gate seems to have arisen either from some mistake, or from ignorance of the practicability of effecting their escape in another direction, for it does not appear that they were aware of General Cooke's situation. The loss of these two parties seems, therefore, to have been the more immediate

OFFICERS OF THE FRENCH INFANTRY

cause, of the failure of the enterprise; for had both these parties been enabled to form a junction with General Cooke, we should still, notwithstanding former losses, have been nearly on an equality, in point of numbers at least with the enemy. As matters now stood, after these two losses, which reduced our force in the place to less than half that of the French, General Cooke appears to have done all that could be expected of a prudent and humane commander, in surrendering to prevent a useless expenditure of life, after withdrawing all he could from the place.

It would appear, in consequence of the delay that occurred before General Cooke entered the place, and the repulse of Colonel Morrice's column, that the plan of the attack had been altered; otherwise it is difficult to account for the proceedings of General Skerret in his attempting to penetrate so far along the ramparts to the left of the entrance of the harbour, with so small a force.

In Sir Thomas Graham's dispatch, (as I have already noticed), it is stated that the right column, under General Skerret, and the left under General Cooke, " were directed to form a junction as soon as possible," and "clear the rampart of opponents." From the latter words it is evident that he meant by the nearest way along the ramparts; consequently, according to this arrangement, General Skerret's column, after entering at the mouth of the harbour, should have proceeded along the ramparts to its right. In this direction, Colonel Carleton had proceeded with 150 men, while General Skerret pushed along the ramparts in the opposite direction; from these circumstances, it is fair to conclude that General Skerret despaired of being able to form a junction with the left column, and therefore wished to force the Steenbergen-gate, and admit the 21st Fusiliers, under Colonel Henry, while Colonel Carleton should form a junction with Colonel Jones.

It is stated in Col. Jones's account that General Skerret attempted to fall back on the reserve at the Waterport-gate but was prevented by the rising of the tide at the entrance of the harbour. Though it would be rash at this distance of time to venture to contradict this statement, I cannot help thinking that he has been misinformed on this point; for, on my joining the party, after opening the Waterport gate, I heard nothing of such an attempt having been made; and if they had still entertained the idea of retiring from their position, I could have easily shown them the way by the foot-bridge across the harbour, where Colonel Muller had sent a company of the Royals from the Waterport-gate.

The party were, when I came to them, at bastion 14, (see details Colonel Jones's account) to which they had just retired from bastion 13, where General Skerret had been wounded and taken prisoner, and they were now commanded by Captain Guthrie of the 33rd Regiment: it was under the orders of the last-mentioned officer that we threw up the log parapet, which was of such use to us during the night. The admirable judgment and coolness displayed by this gallant officer, upon whom the command so unexpectedly devolved, cannot be mentioned in too high terms of commendation.

In concluding my narrative, it will, I trust, be admitted, that however much we may deplore the unfortunate issue of the enterprise, and the unforeseen difficulties which tended to frustrate the best concerted plan of operations, there have been few occasions during the war in which the courage and energies of British soldiers have been put to such a severe test or have been met by a more gallant and successful resistance on the part of the enemy.

Surprise of Bergen-op-Zoom, March, 1814 by Sir John T. Jones of the Royal Engineers

The author was a highly regarded officer and authority on the subject of fortification and siege craft who served under Wellington extensively. To understand the narrative completely readers should refer to the Jones map of Bergen-op-Zoom.

It is very rarely indeed that the bulk of men, whether in professional or civil life, judge correctly of military enterprises. Success almost invariably draws forth their unqualified applause; and failure too generally their reproach, as being the offspring of rashness, imbecility, or misconduct.

The unsuccessful attempt made by Sir Thomas Graham in 1814 to surprise Bergen-op-Zoom has been included in this general sentence of condemnation, to an extent which the occurrences of the night by no means appear to warrant.

This must be imputed to the very slight account of the operation, hitherto published, and the absence of all discussion on its details. During enterprise, however, when judiciously undertaken, adds so much to the force and character of an army, by the energy and confidence it inspires in its ranks, as well as by the distraction and distrust it generates amongst its opponents, and, moreover, is of such rare occurrence, that it becomes almost a national object to uphold any effort which can bear that stamp. It is, therefore, to be hoped that some actor in the scene on the 8th March, fully qualified, will clearly and candidly point out the several causes which led to failure and the capture of the assailants; that any errors of plan or execution may be corrected or avoided in future wars, and one failure be compensated by the success of a hundred similar enterprises.

In the meanwhile, the following compilation from the *Gazette*, the *Narrative* of the French Colonel Le Grand, and notes written on the spot in the summer of 1814, under the eye of the guide who led the columns into the place, is submitted as an attempt to throw some light on those points.

The defences of Bergen-op-Zoom were re-modelled by General Coehorn in 1688, with the view of giving the greatest practicable degree of strength to the right flank of the lines of Steenbergen, at that period regarded as the most valuable defensive barrier of Holland.

As the place had a secure communication with the flotilla, and the garrison could always be relieved or reinforced to any extent from the troops in the lines, the works were traced on a very extensive scale, for the double purpose of better defence, and that the town might be sufficiently capacious to contain supplies for an army.

The details of the fortifications were happily adapted to these peculiarities, and to the nature of the ground, so as to combine great strength with the utmost economy: within the lines of Steenbergen from 13 to 10, their construction is the most simple possible, being merely bastioned fronts with demi-revetments of 16 or 18 feet in height, covered by very low revetted counterscarps, from which revetments the earth rises at an angle of 50° to the summit of the parapet and level of the covered way.

The fronts 1, 2, 3, 4, in rear of Fort d'Eau, being covered by a marsh overflowed at high tide, and having a great command of water defence, were constructed without any revetment; whereas the fronts between the marsh and the lines of Steenbergen, 4 to 9, having but few natural advantages, were constructed with a variety of outworks flanked by galleries for reverse fire in their counterscarps, and were extensively countermined; and further, their right flank was supported by a system of detached lunettes, 16, 17, 18, to obtain for that point a corresponding degree of strength with that given to the left by the lines of Steenbergen.

Thus, under the original view of forming the right of an extensive line of defence, and being always open to maritime succour, as well as being in constant communication with an army in the lines, and therefore assured of an ample garrison, Bergen-op-Zoom justly merited the reputation of a place of the greatest strength, and afforded a good specimen of the art of fortifying; particularly during those happy eras of war, when undisturbed repose in winter quarters invariably repaid the fatigue of a summer's campaign, and left no apprehension for the efficiency of water defences during hard frosts.

Bergen-op-Zoom, however, viewed as a blockaded fortress, with a very inadequate garrison of foreign troops, its maritime communications cut off, the lines of Steenbergen thrown down, the inhabitants disaffected, if not hostile, and a winter of unusual duration, was certainly the weakest possible place, and could not but present an inviting object of enterprise to an enemy.

General Sir Thomas Graham, who commanded a corps of 9000 or 10,000 British troops, disembarked at Willemstadt at the end of 1813, for the purpose of aiding to expel the French garrisons from Holland, justly viewed it in that light; and having reason to believe from the reports of some of the inhabitants who found means of daily egress and ingress, that the garrison little exceeded 2000 men—that the entry into the town by the mouth of the River Zoom, which is nearly dry at low water, was very indifferently guarded—that the ice on the ditches was but partially broken—and that the severe frost would prevent the garrison from using their sluices to raise or lower the ice, or to fill the ditches usually kept dry—decided to attempt to surprise and escalade the place on the night of the 8th March.

The command of the enterprise was intrusted to Major-General Cooke, and the arrangements were for 3300 men to march in three columns from their cantonments and be at their several places of attack at half-past 10 p.m., being the hour of low water.

One column, under Major-General Skerret and Brigadier-General Gore, consisting of 1100 men, was to advance by the Tholen Dyke, and enter the town by the channel of the Zoom, between bastions 1 and 15; then to ascend the rampart of fronts 1, 2, on their right, and advance along it to form a junction with other columns intended to enter by escalade.

Officer of engineers, with this column, Lieutenant Sperling.

A second column, consisting of 1200 men, under Lieutenant-Colonel Morrice, to escalade fronts 9, 10, which being immediately next to the lines of Steenbergen, and covered by a broad inundation, was one of those on a simple trace.

Captain Michell, of the Royal Artillery, volunteered to act as engineer, and accompany this column.

A third column, consisting of 1000 of the Guards, under Colonel Lord Proby, was to march round the right flank of the lunettes of the

General Bizanet

General Jean Jacques Ambert

retrenched camp 17, 18, cross the broad ditch of fronts 3 and 4, on the ice, and mount the unrevetted rampart.

Officers of engineers, Captain Sir G. Hoste and Lieutenant Abbey.

In addition to the above, a false attack by a body of 650 men, under Lieutenant-Colonel Henry, was ordered against bastion 12, (in the right face of which is the Steenbergen gate,) to distract the attention of the garrison.

These several assaults and demonstrations to be made simultaneously.

Such was the plan for the surprise and escalades. The defensive arrangements of General Bizanet, dictated by the peculiar nature of the defences, seemed as if planned expressly to counteract the project of the assailants; for having a very insufficient garrison, (only 2700 effective men under arms,) he kept no force in any of the outworks, except those covering the several gates, where he posted small guards in the retrenchments of the lunettes, to watch the approach to the bridges and gates.

In Fort d'Eau he shut up only sixty men, and to the redoubts of the retrenched camp allotted only twenty men to raise an alarm, should any hostile body approach the unrevetted fronts; and by these excellent arrangements kept nearly the total of his force concentrated under his own hand. Within the fortress, also, he acted on a similar system of concentration; for having established a few small posts in sheltered bivouacs on the ramparts, ready to move in an instant on any point attacked, he directed the remainder of the garrison to assemble, in the event of an alarm, on the weak fronts 11, 12, 13, and in reserve on the place of arms; which, being centrically situated, with direct communications to the gates and rampart, was convenient to succour any point. The field artillery were also to assemble at this spot, or on bastion 12, being the centre of the weak fronts.

On the night of the 8th March, between 9 and 10 o'clock, the officers of the garrison being mostly assembled at General Bizanet's quarters, were called to arms by a sharp musketry fire at the gate of Steenbergen (bastion 12). This was the false attack under Lieutenant-Colonel Henry, which, having fallen unexpectedly on the French guard in the lunette, had bayoneted it, and reached the drawbridge without opposition; and not being provided with instruments of destruction, were endeavouring to open the gate by main force, when discovered from the ramparts.

★★★★★★

The officers of the garrison, at the moment of the alarm, were leaving the cafe in the Square, to join their respective corps: a superior officer desired them to remain until he could communicate with the governor, which he did, and quickly returned, giving them instructions how to act; to this circumstance was, in a great measure, attributed the success of the defence. No time was lost in sending for orders, and each commanding officer knew what he was to do, and acted accordingly.—Communicated to the original editor by a French officer, who was one of the garrison.

★★★★★★

The posts *en bivouac* immediately opened a musketry fire on the assailants, the artillery of the front soon afterwards joined in a general discharge of grape, and the reserves hastened to the spot; when the attacking forces being overwhelmed with every nature of fire, were repulsed with very great loss. In the morning the bodies of many of the assailants, stretched on the top of the demi-revetment, or lying on the sill of the gateway, proved the daring intrepidity with which this attempt had been made.

Immediately after the failure of this bold effort to force the Steenbergen gate, the column under Major-Generals Skerret and Gore, marching along the Tholen Dyke, arrived at the sluice of the inundation undiscovered. They then descended from the dyke to their right, and keeping along the foot of the glacis, entered the mouth of the harbour on a front of six or eight men, and waded in between two and three feet depth of water, along the bed of the Zoom. A guard-boat stationed at the mouth of the harbour fired a shot or two on discovering their approach, and immediately rowed away. The only obstacle the assailants subsequently met with was a number of iron crows' feet scattered over the bottom of the channel, which however failed to arrest their progress for a moment, and the column, about a quarter before 11 o'clock, found itself within the fortress with scarcely a man disabled.

All the reserves of the garrison having been very inconsiderately directed to the Steenbergen gate, on the alarm created by the false attack, no sufficient force could be brought to the harbour in time to oppose the further movements of the assailants, and they, almost unmolested, seized and forced open the Waterport gate in the curtain of fronts 1, 2. Six hundred men were ordered to take post at the gate, to keep open the communication with the exterior, and admit the column ordered to escalade the unrevetted fronts on its left, 2, 3, 4; whilst the right wing of the 44th regiment, about 150 men under Lieut.-Colonel the Honourable George Carleton, should patrol round the rampart to the right; and General Skerret, with a similar force of the same battalion, make a reconnoissance along the rampart of fronts 15, 14, 13, to their left.

This latter small body speedily came in contact with a superior force of the garrison, assembled on the weak fronts, and after a fruitless endeavour to penetrate to bastion 12 (the point of the false attack), fell back to join the troops at the Waterport gate; but, on reaching the mouth of the harbour, found the tide had risen so much that the channel was no longer fordable. General Skerret was consequently separated from all junction with his division, except by the narrow foot-bridge (B) over the harbour in the town, respecting the situation of which he was ignorant; and no alternative remained but to take up the best position he could find on the ramparts. He first selected bastion No. 13, which being partly hollowed out and flanked by a stone windmill, of which he had possession, seemed to offer a good position for inferior numbers to defend themselves. In this bastion, being attacked by a body of infantry, he successfully resisted their efforts, till three fieldpieces with grape-shot were brought up, and made such destruction amongst his men as to induce him to fall back on bastion 14, the gorge of which he barricaded with logs of wood, to serve as a defensive parapet, and enable him to wait the issue of the enterprise.

Lieutenant-Colonel Carleton, with his detachment of the 44th regiment, having made an opening in a row of palisades, which separated the demi-bastion 2 from bastion 3, proceeded along the rampart to his right. The whole of the reserves of the garrison had been most injudiciously again marched in a body to oppose the attack at the mouth of the harbour.

★★★★★★

It was a serious fault thus at once to have disposed of our reserves. The truth is, we all ran to the point which we believed most in danger, and in consequence no one remained to oppose any further effort of an enemy.—*Relation of Colonel Le Grand.*

★★★★★★

Colonel Carleton continued his progress almost unopposed along the fronts 4, 5, 6, 7, and 8, making the small posts of the garrison throw down their arms to bastion 9; when the French troops, coming up in force from their point of concentration on the weak fronts 10, 11, 12, drove him back with considerable loss, till supported by General Gore,

Thelen Dyke

River Zoom

Fort d'Eau

Low Water Mark

St. HELDT

Marshes covered

at high Water

Water Gate

Palisade

14

B

7

2

3

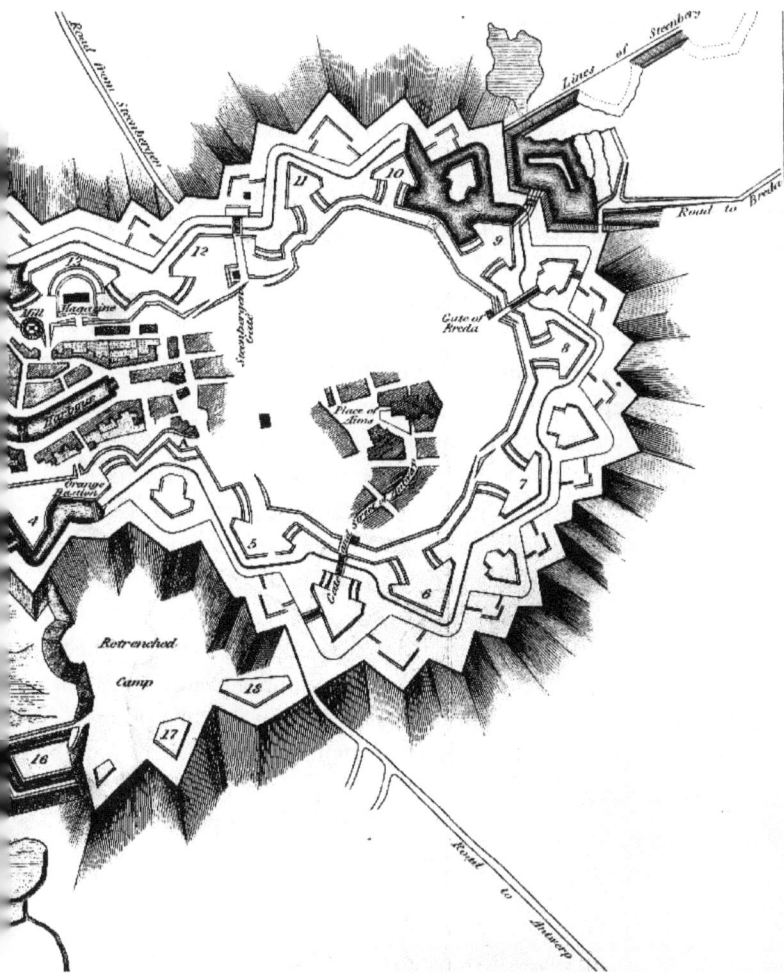

Road from Steenbergen

Lines of Steenbergen

Road to Breda

Road to Breda

12

11

10

9

13

Steenbergen Creek

Gate of Breda

Mill Magazine

8

Palace

Place of Arms

Orange Bastion

7

4

5

6

Retrenched Camp

18

16

17

Road to Antwerp

who had followed his movements along the rampart with other 200 men, and had taken post in bastion 7.

The repulse of Colonel Carleton's force was only just effected by the garrison, when their exertions were called to repel an attack on front 9, 10. This was the column under Lieutenant-Colonel Morrice, which, having found no obstacle to their approach, except a *cunette* in the ice about sixteen feet wide, through which they had readily scrambled, had now reached the glacis.

★★★★★★

In consequence of permission given to the mills to work, which could only be during the falling tide or at low water, the depth of water in the *cunette* in the ditches had been reduced to less than two feet, and the *cunettes* were in reality no obstacle to the approach of an enemy.—*Relation of Colonel Le Grand.*

★★★★★★

On attempting to lower themselves down the counterscarp, they were discovered from the ramparts, and the front being well manned, and everything prepared for resistance, such a heavy fire was poured upon them, that destruction seemed inevitable; nevertheless, the men descended into the ditch, and attempted to rear the ladders against the scarp wall, but after the failure of several gallant efforts, and the loss of nearly 200 men and officers killed and wounded, the senior officer effective ordered the remainder to withdraw out of the ditch and formed them beyond the glacis.

The Guards under Lord Proby, from the Antwerp road, marched round the salient angle of the lunette 16 of the intrenched camp, and reached the broad wet ditch of the unrevetted fronts 2, 3, 4, undiscovered; but after some time spent in vain endeavours to pass over the ditch, finding that the tide affected the ice so as to prevent its bearing their weight, they were under the necessity of changing their point of attack; which they did by edging away to their right till they came to that part of the ditch in rear of the retrenched camp where a *bâtardeau* prevents the tide acting, except by means of the sluices. At that spot the ice was consequently firm, and the ladders being reared against the demi-revetment of the Orange bastion about 17 feet in height, the men entered the place without other resistance than a slight musketry fire from some of the posts overpowered by Colonel Carleton's detachment, which, after he had passed, finding all quiet, had resumed their arms.

General Cooke entered the place with this column; as did the commanding officers of artillery and engineers, Lieutenant-Colonels

116

Sir G. Wood and Smyth.

In consequence of the delay occasioned by Lord Proby having been obliged to change his point of attack as above narrated, it was half-past eleven by the regulated time before this achievement was accomplished, (General Cooke's Dispatch); and General Cooke, concluding from the French posts being at that hour in quiet possession of the defences, that the other columns had not yet entered, formed the Guards on the rampart, occupying also some houses in their front, and the bastions on the right and left of the ladders by which they had escaladed; and which, remaining elevated against the scarp wall, assured the means of constant and ready communication with the exterior. That effected, he sent a strong patrol towards the harbour to gain intelligence of General Skerret's column, and a detachment of 300 men, under Colonel Clifton, to force open the Antwerp gate, and facilitate the entry of the column ordered to escalade the fronts 8 and 9.

******

This is another strong instance of the good effect which might arise, where separate columns of attack are employed on the same enterprise at night, to furnish each with its peculiar signal, either blue-lights, rockets, or parachutes, as a means to communicate its success, or failure, to the other columns.

******

Colonel Clifton, with his detachment, having surprised the French guard, reached the Antwerp gate without loss; and after some strenuous endeavours to force it open, rendered ineffectual from want of means or implements, charged a body of the garrison which were firing on his party from the street of Antwerp: General Gore's detachment from bastion 7 joined in the charge, and the assailants had already captured a field-piece, and were on the point of penetrating to the place of arms, when the French reserves advanced in a body, and completely overpowered them. General Gore, Colonels Clifton and Macdonald, and many officers and men, were killed, and the remainder made prisoners.

A second detachment, under Lieutenant-Colonel Rooke, pushed forward with the same view, forced its way to the Antwerp gate; but finding the gate closed, and the *lunette* in its front occupied, "which being considered to command the bridge, and effectually render the outlet useless," no attempt was made to force open the gate, but the party fell back with some loss.

******

117

This opinion was evidently formed on a misconception of the nature and intent of outworks; they being invariably so constructed as to afford no cover against the fire of the place. Had the party taken with them a petard or case of powder, and blown open the gate, the French guard in the *lunette* would have been completely at their mercy. It does not, however, appear from the subsequent transactions, that forcing open the gate would have been of any utility, as Colonel Morrice's column entered by the ladders, and the communication with the exterior was by the same means kept free throughout the night.

★★★★★★

About this time the remnant of Lieutenant-Colonel Morrice's column, (except a party of 150 left to remove the wounded,) having marched round the foot of the glacis, entered the place by the ladders of Lord Proby's column, and formed on the rampart to the left of the Guards.

General Cooke being still very imperfectly acquainted with the events which had occurred, and with the positions of the other assaulting columns, and finding that every detachment he sent out was either cut off or beaten back with loss, decided on this augmentation of his force to keep it together in a body, so as to maintain a position on the Orange and adjacent bastions, which should cover his communication with the exterior by means of the ladders, and admit of reinforcements to any extent being introduced for his support; or till daylight should enable him to ascertain the force and position of the garrison, so as to decide how best to direct his further efforts for their capture. Captain Sir G. Hoste was sent out by the ladders, to communicate these views and intentions to the commander of the forces.

The respective situations of the two parties, about one o'clock on the morning of the 9th, were as follows.

The weather clear and bright, but extremely cold.

ASSAILANTS.

1. At the Waterport gate	600
2. Detachment in bastions 14, 15, under General Skerret	120
3. General Cooke's column at the Orange bastion, deducting the detachment prisoners, and other losses	650
4. Column which had failed to escalade bastion 9, one wing of the 55th being left to remove wounded, and deducting losses during the attempt to assault	900
	2270

Formed on the ramparts, and only waiting for daylight to follow up and complete their brilliant achievements; but being spread over twelve of the sixteen fronts of the place, and in three separate bodies, the strongest of which only mustered 1550 men, and in perfect ignorance of all the localities.

GARRISON.

About the same number of men as the assailants, in momentary expectation of being overpowered; but formed so as to support each other principally en masse, on the place of arms in the centre of the town, or on the fronts 9, 10, 11, 12, and having a perfect knowledge of all the communications, and of everything around them favourable to their defence.

★★★★★★

Colonel Le Grand, who had every motive of vanity and nationality for calculating the force of the garrison at the lowest amount possible, states the number of men under arms at the commencement of the assault to have been 2700: they may, therefore, be supposed at this period to have been 2400 or 2500 men.

★★★★★★

In this state of things the capture of the place was deemed so inevitable by the assailants, that a brigade of German troops, which on hearing the firing had advanced from Tholen, countermarched; the detachment which had made the false attack returned to its cantonments, the commanding officers of artillery and engineers withdrew, and the principal guide, who had proposed the enterprise and conducted the columns, even carried his confidence so far as to return to his house in the town, and retire to bed.

Nevertheless, the night being bitterly cold, the troops, after remaining for two or three hours in the same positions, became weary and impatient: that daring courage which bade defiance to open danger, and was equal to triumph over every human foe, chilled under the influence of cold, inaction, and suspense; and with some few, despondency and distrust succeeded to animation and confidence.

The garrison, on the contrary, during this long interval of quiet, had in some measure recovered from their first feelings of surprise, and being well acquainted with every locality, were able, before the dawn of day, to feel their way. They first patrolled towards the mouth of the harbour along the berm of the demi-revetment of bastions 13,

14, 15, and then on other points, till having fully ascertained the separation of the assailants, they decided to commence the offensive, with their whole force, on the first dawn of day.

In pursuance of this plan, about 6 a.m. on the 9th, they commenced with General Skerret's small party in bastion 14; and which, "left to their own resources, defended themselves with a degree of intelligence and obstinacy of which history offers Zoom few examples." (Words of Colonel Le Grand's *Relation*.) Being attacked by four times their number with field-pieces, they continued to shelter themselves behind their log retrenchments, and give battle with the heavy guns of the place, till a party of French, directed along the berm, mounted the parapet of the faces of the bastion, and unexpectedly falling on their rear, diverted their efforts, and caused them to be overpowered.

The garrison next directed their main strength against the 600 men formed near the Waterport gate and poured such a fire upon them from the ramparts of 15, the arsenal, and surrounding buildings, as to drive the men for shelter through the gateway. In that situation, finding themselves immediately under view of a whole front, it was decided to withdraw; but no officer being sufficiently acquainted with the details of fortification to point out the sure retreat which the covered-way of fronts 2, 3, 4 presented to their view, they crowded into the *caponière* of communication to Fort d'Eau, the guns of which work immediately opened upon them. The successful party soon afterwards manned the guns of the main rampart; when the retiring force, finding themselves shut in between two fires, laid down their arms.

General Cooke, on learning there was a serious affair near the Waterport gate, was induced to detach a battalion along the rampart, to take part in the struggle. This battalion, on approaching the spot, finding the gateway in the possession of the garrison, the English detachment prisoners, and a strong body of French preparing to advance against them, mounted on the parapet, and from thence descending the exterior slope of the unrevetted fronts 2, 3, 4, quitted the place by crossing the broad ditch of those fronts on the ice, losing, however, several men, who broke through and were drowned.

The French having now cleared the ramparts of all the assailants except the force under General Cooke on the Orange bastion, (reduced by casualties, and detaching a battalion, to 1000 to 1200 men,) united all their strength in a combined movement against that point. The column from the Waterport gate formed in bastion 5 to attack their left flank, whilst another column should attack their right, and the remainder of the garrison direct a fire of artillery and musketry on their front. The column from No. 5 advanced in gallant style, and penetrated to the point A, where they were met by so warm a fire of musketry and of the artillery of the bastion, that they dispersed, and were driven back with loss into No. 5 bastion: at this time, the French column from the right opened a fire both of musketry and field artillery, seconded by an equally galling fire of musketry and heavy guns from various points of the rampart, and of *tirailleurs* from every spot which afforded cover in their front.

★★★★★★

We did not fire during the whole night a single musket from the houses, for this simple reason, that we never occupied any; and it was this forbearance which caused our strength. It is, however, probable that the guards, during the darkness, mistook a firing from the ramparts behind the houses for a firing from within the houses.—Note to *Relation par le Chevalier Le Grand*.

★★★★★★

The troops stood firm and replied to this galling fire with much coolness from the rampart and the Zoom houses in its front, till General Cooke, finding that he was losing many men with little chance of ultimately maintaining his post, determined, on the suggestion of the officer commanding the party, to let the troops withdraw by the ladders; which they commenced with the utmost coolness and regularity. During this operation the French, with the view of cutting off the communication with the exterior, possessed themselves of various points flanking the wall against which the ladders were reared, and opened a fire of grape from the flank guns on the men descending the ladders.

They were, however, speedily dislodged by a gallant charge with the bayonet by Majors Muttlebury and Hogg, of the 55th, and the evacuation of the place by the ladders continued steadily in progress, when a summons to surrender was received from General Bizanet, accompanied by an officer who had been made prisoner in the night. General Cooke learnt from this unimpeachable source the surrender of the troops at the Waterport gate, the loss of Colonel Clifton's and General Skerret's detachments, and the fall of Brigadier-General Gore and Lieutenant-Colonel Carleton; and also that the French had brought up and placed combustibles to burn the houses occupied as advanced posts by his column. This disastrous intelligence made him feel that a longer continuance of the struggle, situated as he was, without any immediate prospect of being reinforced, would be an useless expenditure of life; and, in consequence, he assented to the mortifying conditions of surrendering himself and troops prisoners of war.

In this protracted defence the garrison had 460 killed or wounded, and being reduced to little more than 2200 effectives, delivered up by a convention next morning 1800 British prisoners.

Notwithstanding this ultimate failure, it is impossible to read the foregoing narrative without admitting the utmost ability to have been displayed by the officers, and the most spirited conduct and determined bravery to have been evinced by the troops in following up the plans of their commander; which, thus supported, were so far successful as to establish a hostile force in superior numbers to the garrison on the ramparts of the town: nor can we but admire the steady discipline and excellent order so long maintained by the assailants in that trying situation during the obscurity of night, and whilst surrounded by the almost irresistible temptations of plunder and liquor.

Such daring conduct, combined with such discipline, creates a high feeling of respect for the British soldiery, and a full conviction that, with such instruments, the attempt to surprise Bergen-op-Zoom was both feasible and judicious, under the circumstances of the moment; and it must ever be a subject of regret that too divided a plan of operations, coupled with some minor errors of execution and arrangement, should have converted early triumph into ultimate defeat, and snatched a splendid and well-merited prize from the grasp of Sir Thomas Graham.

Expedition to Holland, 1813-14 (Bergen-op-Zoom)

'Intelligence Branch Officer'

INTRODUCTION BY THE LEONAUR EDITORS

This account is taken from a small publication published in 1884 entitled, British Minor Expeditions, 1746 to 1814. The actual authors are not given though implicitly each account (the work contains eleven accounts) was potentially the work of a different contributor. The book was a British Government publication printed for Her Majesty's Stationery Office stating that the contents had been compiled in the Intelligence Branch of the Quartermaster-General's Department. The short introduction of this work informs us that, 'each short account had been drawn up during intervals of more serious work by officers employed in the Intelligence Branch without any view to publication without any claim to originality, being for the most part compilations from well-known authorities'. Be that as it may, this source is today recognised as one of the most reliable and authoritative on the subject of Bergen-op-zoom in 1814.

In the year 1813 the people of Holland determined to throw off the French yoke and regain their national independence under the rule of the Prince of Orange. The British Government having resolved to aid the Dutch in this attempt, a force for the purpose was despatched to the coast of Holland, under the command of Sir Thomas Graham, afterwards Lord Lynedoch.

Troops were embarked at various times during the months of November and December, 1813, with this view, at Ramsgate, Dover, and Harwich, arriving in Holland by brigades, single battalions, or detachments, at the following places:—Scheveling (or Scheveningen), Hellevoetsluis, Stevenisse (Island of Tholen), and Willemstadt

By the 27th of December, 1813, the different portions of the troops were concentrated in cantonments about Klundert, Willemstadt, and Zeevenbergen; the force being organised in brigades as follows:—

Bergen op Zoom in the 18th Century

				Nominal strength.
Guards' Brigade, Major-General Cooke.	1st Regiment 2nd (Coldstreams) 3rd „			1,600
Light Brigade, Major-General Mackenzie.	35th „ 2nd battalion 52nd „ 2nd „ 73rd „ 2nd „ 95th „ 3rd „			1,900
1st Brigade, Major-General Skerrett.	37th „ 2nd „ 44th „ 2nd „ 55th „ 69th „ 2nd „ 1st Veteran Battalion			2,500
2nd Brigade, Major-General Gibbs.	25th Regiment, 2nd battalion 33rd „ 54th „ 56th „ 3rd battalion			2,060
	5 companies of Artillery			615
			Total	8,675

Note.—The battalions of the 25th, 33rd, 54th, and 73rd regiments had just returned from Swedish Pomerania, under Major-General Gibbs, and on reaching Yarmouth Roads were sent to Holland without landing.

The officers of the force were for the most part young and inexperienced men, whilst the greater portion of the rank and file were mere boys unfit for the hardships of a campaign.

During the first week of the new year the 2nd King's German Hussars, and on the 10th January the 2nd battalions of the 21st and 78th Regiments, arrived in Holland, the 21st being placed in the 1st Brigade, replacing the Veteran Battalion, which was left as a garrison at various places, and the 78th in the 2nd Brigade.

General von Bülow, who commanded the 3rd Prussian Corp d'Armée, the most advanced portion of the armies about to invade France, had his headquarters at Bommel.

The French held various fortified towns in Holland and Flanders, amongst others Bergen-op-Zoom and Antwerp; they also had troops from Wustwezel, north-east of the latter place, on the Breda- Antwerp road, by Hoogstraeten, Turnhout, to Eindhoven.

General von Bülow, at the beginning of January, determined to advance southwards from Breda, breaking through the French line at Hoogstraeten and Wustwezel, thus cutting off the detachments of the enemy to the eastward of these places; and further to make a reconnaissance of Antwerp, and carry it if possible by a *coup de main*.

Sir Thomas Graham, to assist in this operation, was to advance southwards on the right of the Prussian line of attack, and, if possible, get between the French at Hoogstraeten and the fortress of Antwerp.

The British headquarters had been advanced as far south as Calmhout (or Calmpthout), a little west of the Breda-Antwerp road.

A force of infantry some 1,200 strong, with a portion of the 2nd King George's Hussars, was left at Wouw to observe Bergen-op-Zoom.

After providing garrisons for Tholen and Willemstadt, the available force for an advance numbered about 4,500 infantry, two squadrons of the 2nd King George's Hussars, and two field batteries (twelve guns).

The army was now organised in two divisions, each having a battery of artillery attached to it, as follows:—

1st Division, Major-General Coote.	Guards' Brigade, Colonel Lord Proby. 1st Brigade, Major-General Skerrett.
2nd Division, Major-General Mackenzie.	Light Brigade, Major-General Gibbs. 2nd Brigade, Major-General Taylor.

On the morning of the 11th January the Prussians advanced and drove back the French from about Hoogstraeten and Westwezel as far as Braeschaet, on the Breda-Antwerp road. During the night the French drew back their line closer to Antwerp, their left resting on the village of Merxem.

The British and Prussians continued to push on their advance; the former, on the evening of that day, having the 1st Division at Capelle, the 2nd at Eckeren in front of Merxem.

The Prussians had reached Braeschaet the same night, their right having advanced by the Breda-Antwerp road, the British keeping to the west of that road.

On the 13th the French were driven in on the fortress by a combined attack of the British and Prussian troops.

The English share of the engagement was the capture of the village of Merxem, which was carried by the 2nd Division after some sharp fighting.

The loss suffered by the division was: killed, 1 officer and 9 rank and file; wounded, 4 officers and 25 rank and file. 25 rank and file of the enemy were taken prisoners.

General von Bülow, finding the fortress too strong to be taken by a *coup de main*, and not deeming it practicable to invest the place on account of the severity of the weather, determined to retire again into cantonments in and about Breda.

The British also retired northwards, the 1st Division being cantoned about Eschen and Nispen, the 2nd at Calmhout.

Towards the end of the month, General von Bülow acceded to the desire of Sir T. Graham to make another advance on Antwerp, and to attempt to destroy, by a bombardment, the fleet lying in the basin there.

On the 31st January, 1814, the Prussian headquarters had been moved to Westmalle; the British troops, having a strength of about 6,000 infantry, had their headquarters at Brecht, the 1st Division being at Wustwezel and Louenhout, the 2nd at Brecht.

The British troops had advanced as far south as Braeschaet on the evening of the 1st February, and on the morning of the next day the village of Merxem was again attacked and carried, although it had been considerably strengthened by the French since the former attack on it.

The village was earned by the 2nd Division, who captured there two guns and a few prisoners.

Under cover of his own troops in the front and supported by the Prussians on the left, Sir T. Graham proceeded to erect batteries for the bombardment of the fleet.

By the afternoon of the 3rd February the batteries opened fire, being armed with twelve English pieces (24-pounder guns), howitzers, and mortars, and thirteen Dutch mortars of various calibres.

This day's fire disabled most of the Dutch mortars.

At noon on the 4th, fire was again commenced with seventeen pieces of artillery; and was resumed on the 5th with the same number of guns, the bombardment lasting till sunset.

During these three days' bombardment, the ships, having had their decks covered with timber and turf, were not much damaged, except about the spars, two only of them being disabled.

The French made several attempts to carry the batteries, coming from the east of the fortress, but were driven back by the Prussian troops. The losses suffered by the British at the second taking of Merxem, and during the three days' bombardment, were: killed, 9 rank and file; wounded, 17 officers, 11 sergeants, 4 drummers and 169 rank and file.

The enemy lost 180 prisoners to the British.

Whilst this bombardment was going on, General von Bülow received orders to advance southwards into France to co-operate with the Grand Army, then entering France from the south and east.

On 6th February Sir Thomas Graham withdrew his troops and guns from their positions in front of Antwerp, and retired northwards, again into cantonments.

On the 10th his forces were disposed as follows:—

Headquarters at Groot Zundert.

1st Division about Rozendaal.

2nd Division about Groot Zoondert, having two battalions and

127

two guns at Louenhout and Wustwezel. The cavalry (three squadrons 2nd King George's Hussars) being spread out from Wouw and Eschen on the west, to Louenhout and Brecht on the south.

After the advance of General von Bülow in the direction of the French frontier, Sir Thomas Graham was not in sufficient force to attempt anything by himself against Antwerp, and therefore withdrew his line closer to Willemstadt, where all his stores, &c., were deposited, with the object of waiting an opportunity to undertake operations against the fortress of Bergen-op-Zoom, the occupation of which by the French prevented him moving southwards to co-operate with a force of Prussians and Saxons, then occupying the south of Holland, and which had advanced as far as Brussels.

In the beginning of February, the 3rd King George's Hussars; the 4th battalion Royal Scots, and the 2nd battalion 91st Regiment arrived in Holland, having marched from Stralsund, and the 2nd battalions of the 30th and 81st Regiments landed from England, making an increase of force of 2,100 bayonets.

At this period, the French having again appeared in force about Courtrai, the Duke of Saxe-Weimar, commanding a corps of Saxon troops then investing Maubeuge, informed Sir Thomas Graham that a corps of some 3,000 infantry and a body of cavalry had started from Cambrai to reinforce Antwerp; the latter, therefore, moved the right of his corps, on the 4th March, southwards to Stabroek and Putten, to prevent any reinforcement reaching Bergen-op-Zoom from Antwerp, and fixed his headquarters at Calmpthout.

The arrival of a body of Russian seamen to garrison the island of Tholen, &c., set free some of Sir Thomas Graham's force hitherto engaged on that duty.

On the night of the 8th March an assault was made on the fortress of Bergen-op-Zoom, of which place the following is a description, taken from Cust's *Wars of the Nineteenth Century*.

> Before the gate of Antwerp is a large redoubt joining the fortified lines called Kijkin-de-Pot, strengthened by four flanking forts armed with cannon. On the side of the Steenbergen are the forts of Moermont, Pinsen and Rover, with a well-fortified line of connection, beyond which is an inundation reaching all the way to the Steenbergen. Before the Water-gate is a regular fort of five bastions called Zuyd Schants, under cover of which two canals lead from the Schelde and form the harbour. On the

east towards Breda is another considerable inundation caused by the waters of the Zoom, which renders the whole approach on that side marshy and inaccessible. The body of the place is defended by a rampart about a league in circumference, flanked by ten bastions, covered by six horn-works; in addition to which an extensive system of mines and subterraneous galleries render every approach to the fortress hazardous in the extreme.

Bergen-op-Zoom was a strongly fortified place, but having a very weak garrison, 2,800 men only, the length of its line of defences was a source of weakness; moreover, the ditches being unrevetted, and the scarps having crumbled away from the effects of the frost, made the passage of them comparatively easy.

Sir Thomas Graham, learning from some Dutch officers who had recently been in the place, and were well acquainted with it and its garrison, that it could be entered at three points with ease, and that the morale of the garrison was very poor, determined to make an effort to carry the place by assault.

The attack was organised in four columns, taken from the troops of the 1st Division; the 2nd Division to furnish a supporting force, and to observe Antwerp during the carrying out of the plan.

The first column was made up of—

> 600 stormers.
> 400 supports.
> —

Total, 1,000 men, from the Guards' brigade, under the command of Colonel Lord Proby.

This column was ordered to move from Hoogerheide to Borgvliet, and from thence to enter the place between the southern or Antwerp gate, and the north-western or Water-gate.

On gaining the ramparts, the column was to move to its left to form a junction with No. 4 column, which was to enter by the Water-gate.

The second column consisted of—

Stormers:
> 55th Regiment 250
> 69th   ,,   350
Supports:
> 33rd   ,,   600
> —

Total, 1,200 men, under the command Lieutenant-

Colonel Morrice, 69th Regiment.

This column was to move from Huibergen to the north of the eastern or Wouw gate, with orders on gaining the ramparts to communicate to its left with No. 1 column, and to act according to circumstances.

The third column was destined only to make a false attack, ready to co-operate with the others if successful, and consisted of—

21st Regiment	100
37th „	150
91st „	400

Total, 650 men, under command of Lieutenant-Colonel Henry, 21st Regiment. This column was to advance from Halsteren towards the north or Steenbergen gate. The fourth column consisted of—

$$\text{Flank companies}\begin{cases}\text{44th regiment,} & 300 \\ \begin{cases}\text{21st } & \text{\textit{„}} \\ \text{37th } & \text{\textit{„}}\end{cases}200 \\ \text{1st Royal Scots,} & 600\end{cases}\begin{matrix}\text{stormers.}\\ \\ \text{supports.}\end{matrix}$$

Total, 1,100 men, under command of Lieutenant-Colonel Carleton, 44th regiment. This column was to move from Halsteren by the junction of the two dykes to the north-west of the town, and fording the Zoom stream (widened and deepened at this part into a tidal canal, passable at low water), to enter the place by the Water-gate

On gaining the ramparts it was to move to its right and form a junction with No. 1 column.

The total strength of the four columns was 3,950 rank and file.

Each column was guided by a selected officer, having a party of sappers and miners under his command.

Major-General Cooke accompanied the first column, Major-General Skerrett and Brigadier-General Gore being with No. 4 column.

In order to distinguish friends from foes in the darkness and confusion, the men were instructed on the approach of any one to call out "*Orange Boven*" (Up with the Orange) the answer to which challenge was to be "God save the King."

As No. 4 column had to ford the Zoom, and it was low water about 10 p.m. on the 8th March, that hour was chosen for the simultaneous attack of all the columns.

The false attack. No. 3 column, opened fire between 9 and 10 p.m., and took the guard by surprise, but was stopped at the drawbridge by the fire from the place, and retired, suffering severely. The sound of musketry, nevertheless, attracted the greater portion of the garrison to that side.

No. 4 column was the first to enter the place, forcing the Watergate and clearing the ramparts of the few enemy found there; instead, however, of moving to the right, according to their instructions, they scattered right and left along the ramparts on either side of the gate. While in this disorder they were attacked by the greater portion of the garrison under the *commandant*. General Bizanet, and were very severely handled, General Gore and Colonel Carleton being killed, and General Skerrett receiving a mortal wound. On the fall of their leaders the troops fell into entire confusion, and were made prisoners by the French,

The first column was delayed in its attack by having to change its direction at the last moment, as it was found impracticable to pass the ditch at the indicated spot. However, about 11.30 p.m. the column got into the Orange bastion to the westward of the Antwerp gate, under a galling fire from the few defenders at that part.

On reaching the rampart General Cooke halted, and instead of moving to the left in accordance with his orders, sent only a strong patrol to gain intelligence of the fourth column, but the patrol unfortunately fell into the hands of the enemy. A few houses in front of the column were occupied, and a detachment of the 1st Guards, under Lieutenant-Colonel Clifton, was sent to the right to attempt to open the Antwerp gate, and gain intelligence of No. 3 column; this detachment also fell into the hands of the enemy, who got between it and the Orange bastion.

A detachment of the 3rd Guards, under Lieutenant-Colonel Rooke, was shortly afterwards sent on a similar errand, but could not force its way up the street leading to the Antwerp gate, and found also that an outwork commanding the bridge at that gate was occupied by the enemy, the fire from which would have prevented any entrance at that point.

The second column was arrested in its advance at the glacis by the fire from the main body of the place: its leader, Lieutenant-Colonel Morrice, having been wounded, as also Lieutenant-Colonel Elphinstone, 33rd Regiment, the command devolved upon Major Muttlebury, 69th Regiment, who marched the column round to the left on the outside of the place, leaving a wing of the 55th Regiment to collect the wounded on the glacis. This column then followed No. 1

column on to the Orange bastion.

Whilst General Cooke had been waiting at the Orange bastion the fate of the stormers of No. 4 column had been decided, and when the men of No. 2 column reached the rampart, he sent the 33rd Regiment to the assistance of the men at the Water-gate, but they came too late; part of the regiment succeeded in joining the support of No. 4 column (the Royal Scots), which held its ground at the Water-gate, a portion inside and a portion outside the gate. The French, leaving a part of their force to hold the men at the Water-gate in check by the fire of the guns which they had turned on them, now attacked General Cooke's party on both flanks. Getting into a bastion adjacent to the Orange bastion, they turned the guns on the men of Nos. 1 and 2 columns; but were driven out by a bayonet charge of the wing of the 55th under Major Hog, and the 69tb under Major Muttlebury. By this time day had broken. Guns having been turned on the men on the exposed rampart, General Cooke determined to withdraw, and a portion of the Guards managed to get out of the place; whilst they were leaving, the enemy again entered the bastion next the Orange bastion and were again driven out by a charge of the 55th and 69th Regiments.

Finding he could not effect his retreat, General Cooke yielded to the summons of a French officer, who had come accompanied by Colonel Jones, 1st Guards, a prisoner and who told the general the fate of No. 4 column.

At daylight the Royal Scots, who had been exposed to a galling fire all night, and now stood with the swollen Zoom behind them, laid down their arms, and, together with part of the 33rd Regiment, were made prisoners.

Just as the troops had all surrendered the supports of the 2nd Division arrived outside the place, too late.

The losses in killed and wounded were as follows:—

				Killed.	Wounded.
Officers	..	..	..	17	54
Sergeants	..	..	..	29	28
Drummers	..	..	..	12	7
Rank and File	..	..	..	329	444
	Total	..	..	381	533

Taken prisoners: Officers, 93; sergeants, 93; drummers, rank and file, 1,891. Total of all ranks, 2,077, many of whom were wounded.

The cause of this disaster was the failure of the officers in command of the various columns to carry out the orders they had received.

The fourth column encountered at first scarcely any resistance and would probably have been able to have formed a junction with No. 1 column before the enemy attacked it in any force; or even if attacked before such a junction, it would have been in a better position to resist the onslaught of the French as a collected body than as a set of straggling detachments, and further, would have been within easy support from No. 1 column, when that column did penetrate the place.

Had General Cooke marched to his left according to his orders, instead of only sending a strong patrol in that direction, there seems no doubt that No. 4 column, reinforced by No. 1, could have successfully repelled the French attack, and the arrival of No. 3 column must have made the assault a success.

The garrison was about 2,800 strong, a portion of which would have been occupied at first with Nos. 2 and 3 columns; their attacking force, therefore, would not have exceeded by much the strength of Nos. 1 and 4 columns united, and when No. 3 arrived they would have been considerably outnumbered. Even at the eleventh hour, had the battalion of the Royal Scots held out, it is probable that on the arrival of the troops of the 2nd Division the place might still have been carried.

In a letter from Sir Thomas Graham to Lord Bathurst, dated Calmhout, 11th March, 1814, he says:

> In short, the attack must have succeeded had the orders been obeyed. . . . We had considerable reinforcements at hand soon after daylight from the 2nd Division, when I had the mortification of seeing that they came too late. Still, had the Royals maintained the Water Post Gate, General Cooke would have held his ground, and the place must have fallen."

To whom the blame attaches for the late arrival of the men of the 2nd Division there is nothing to show.

On the 9th March the English prisoners were marched out of Bergen-op-Zoom to the island of Tholen, and after a time were embarked for England, on condition that they should not serve again against France until an equal number of French prisoners in England had been exchanged. Three French officers and 119 men, made prisoners by the force under Sir T. Graham, were sent into Bergen-op-Zoom, a similar number of English prisoners being sent back in exchange.

After the repulse at Bergen-op-Zoom the troops retired into cantonments, investing Bergen, and preparing to invest Antwerp.

On the 21st March Fort Lillo was taken, with the loss of six killed and wounded.

Preparations were made to attack Fort Bath, in the island of South Beveland; but before they were completed, an armistice was agreed upon between Sir Thomas Graham and General Carnot, the Governor of Antwerp, the restoration of the Bourbons and the downfall of Napoleon having changed the aspect of affairs.

In accordance with the Convention of Paris of April 23rd, 1814, the city of Antwerp was occupied by British troops, the 2nd Division and the 1st Brigade of the 1st Division going into cantonments there and garrisoning the various forts on the 5th May.

Shortly after this a portion of the British troops were marched to Brussels, and Sir Thomas Graham, now Lord Lynedoch, was placed in command of the various forces in Flanders, *viz.*: Prussian, Russian, Hanoverian, Swedish, Danish, Dutch, and Belgian, in addition to the British troops.

During the months of June and July, a force of Hanoverian troops in British pay arrived in Flanders, numbering some 3,000 bayonets and sabres. In the month of July, the Prince of Orange assumed command of the forces in Holland and Flanders, Lord Lynedoch returning to England.

The troops remained in various garrisons and cantonments in Holland and Flanders, being reinforced by British, King's German Legion, Hanoverian, and newly raised Dutch and Belgian corps, until the next year, when most of them took part in the Battle of Waterloo.